VISUAL HAMMER

Nail your brand into the mind with the emotional power of a visual

LAURA RIES

OTHER BOOKS BY LAURA RIES

Battlecry (Fall 2015)

OTHER BOOKS BY AL RIES & LAURA RIES

The 22 Immutable Laws of Branding

The 11 Immutable Laws of Internet Branding

The Fall of Advertising & the Rise of PR

The Origin of Brands

War in the Boardroom

Visit Ries.com for more information.

ISBN: 0-9849370-6-4
ISBN-13: 978-0-9849370-6-6

Dedicated to Al Ries,

my hero, mentor, partner and dad

CONTENTS

Preface	By Al Ries.	9
Chapter 1	HAMMER: Its astonishing power.	15
Chapter 2	NAIL: The ultimate objective.	25
Chapter 3	SHAPE: Simple is better.	33
Chapter 4	COLOR: Be the opposite.	43
Chapter 5	PRODUCT: The ideal hammer.	61
Chapter 6	PACKAGE: Make it different.	73
Chapter 7	ACTION: More effective than stills.	83
Chapter 8	FOUNDER: Natural-born hammers.	89
Chapter 9	SYMBOL: Visualizing the invisible.	103
Chapter 10	CELEBRITY: Pros & cons.	115
Chapter 11	ANIMAL: Anthropopathy works.	125
Chapter 12	HERITAGE: Putting the past to work.	143
Chapter 13	YOUR HAMMER: How to find one.	153
	Laura Ries: About the author.	161

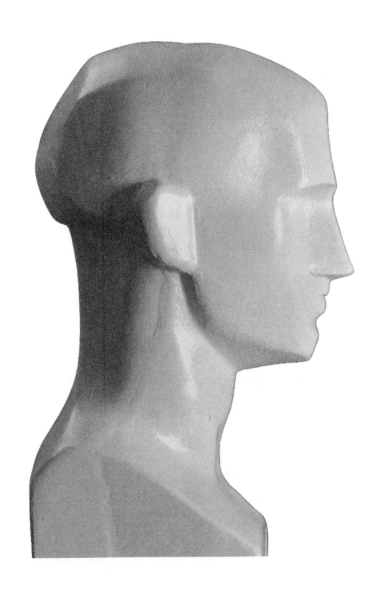

PREFACE
BY AL RIES

Forty-three years ago, Advertising Age published a series of articles I wrote with Jack Tout entitled "The Positioning Era Cometh."

And nine years later, McGraw-Hill published our book "Positioning: The Battle for Your Mind." In the years that followed, "positioning" became one of the most talked-about concepts in marketing. (In 2001, McGraw-Hill released a 20th anniversary edition.)

To date, more than 1.5 million copies of the Positioning book have been sold, including more than 400,000 copies in China alone.

Forty-three years is a long time for any idea to remain relevant, especially in the fast-changing world of marketing. By now, positioning is probably obsolete. Or is it?

Many companies still write positioning statements for their brands. Many marketing programs call for establishing positions in consumers' minds. Many marketing executives still talk in positioning terms.

As recently as the year 2009, the readers of Advertising Age selected "Positioning: The Battle for Your Mind" as the best book they ever read on the subject of marketing.

That was the same year that the Harvard Business School Press published a book entitled "The 100 Best Business Books of All Time." (Positioning was one of the 100 best.)

Authors are still writing books on the subject. In the past few years, "Positioning the Brand," "Competitive Positioning," and "Positioning for Professionals" were published.

Positioning seems to be still important in spite of the many radical changes that have taken place in the field of marketing in the last four decades.

These include: The Internet, social networking, mobile marketing, big data and the rise of PR. Then there's Google, Facebook, LinkedIn, Twitter and dozens of other digital ways to influence consumers.

As important and as revolutionary as these developments are, they are still tactics. And to be successful, a brand needs more than the latest tactic. A brand also needs a strategy and that's why positioning continues to attract attention in the marketing community.

Yet the positioning concept has a weakness. Invariably, positioning strategy is expressed verbally.

In executing a positioning strategy, you look for a verbal hole in the mind and then you try to fill that hole with your brand name.

Lexus, for example, filled a hole called "Japanese luxury vehicle." Once the Lexus brand was securely positioned in consumers' minds, it was almost invulnerable to competition.

In spite of the successes of "verbal" positioning strategies, it may come as a surprise to some readers that the best way into a human mind is not with words at all. It's with visuals.

In 1973, psychology professor Lionel Standing conducted a research study in which he asked subjects to look at 10,000 images over a five-day period. Each image was presented for five seconds each.

When the research subjects were showed pairs of images (one they had seen before and one they had not), they remembered 70 percent of the images they had seen.

That statistic is phenomenal. Try presenting 10,000 positioning slogans for five seconds each and see how many of them a person will remember five days later.

In today's over-communicated society, consumers will remember very few positioning slogans. No matter how cleverly constructed or how well your positioning concept tests in focus groups, if consumers can't remember your message, then all is for naught.

What verbal messages stick in consumers' minds?

What's the glue that holds some concepts in a person's memory for years, even decades?

Emotion.

Think about your past. What events do you remember the most?

Those events that raised your pulse rate and your blood pressure. Those events that were emotional.

The day that you got married. The day your daughter got married. The day you had your car accident.

The day you got promoted. The day you bought your first house. These are all events that you can "picture" in your mind.

Visuals have an emotional power that printed words or aural sounds do not have. Observe people in a theater watching a movie. Quite often they will laugh out loud, sometimes even cry.

Now observe a person reading a novel, perhaps the same novel the motion picture was based on. Seldom will you see outward signs of emotional involvement.

That's the difference between visuals on a screen and printed words in a book. One is emotional; the other is not.

Emotion is the glue that sticks a memory in the mind. But why are visuals emotional and words are not? It's because every brain is actually two brains. A left hemisphere and a right hemisphere.

Your left hemisphere processes information in series. It thinks in language. It works linearly and methodically. Your right hemisphere is different.

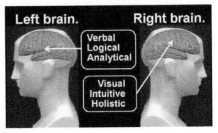

It processes information in parallel. It thinks in mental images. It "sees" the big picture.

Everybody has two brains. One verbal brain and one visual brain.

While the objective of a positioning program is to put a word or a verbal concept into consumers' minds, the best way to do that is not with words at all. It's with a visual that has emotional appeal.

But not just any visual. After all, advertising and other forms of communication are loaded with visual images.

What a brand needs is a visual that reinforces its verbal positioning concept. The visual attracts the attention of the right side of the brain which sends a message to the left side of the brain to read or listen to the words associated with the visual.

The "position," a verbal concept, is the nail. The tool that hammers the positioning nail into consumers' minds is the visual hammer.

That's Laura's idea and I fully expect her Visual Hammer concept to become as famous as Positioning ever was.

1

HAMMER

ITS ASTONISHING POWER.

In the world of business today, the printed word reigns supreme. Tweets, status updates, text messages, bullet points on PowerPoint slides, emails, even old-fashioned letters.

Ideas, projects, reports, agendas and marketing programs are all spelled out in a blizzard of words.

When it comes to executing a marketing program, no wonder business executives focus on the words alone.

Words are what business executives use the most and are the most familiar with. Yet there is a lot of evidence that visuals play a far more important role in marketing than do words.

In 1982, Nancy Brinker started a foundation to fight breast cancer in memory of her sister, Susan G. Komen, who had died from the disease two years earlier. Back then, Brinker says, her only assets were $200 in cash and a list of names of potential donors.

Since then, Susan G. Komen for the Cure has raised more than $2 billion. Today it has become the world's-largest non-profit source of money to combat breast cancer.

In a recent Harris poll of nonprofit brands, consumers rated Komen for the Cure as the charity they were "Most likely to donate to." Ahead of such organizations as American Cancer Society, St. Jude's Research Hospital, Goodwill Industries and the

Salvation Army. What accounts for the amazing success of a nonprofit organization with the longest and strangest name in the field?

It's the pink ribbon which has become a well-known symbol in the fight against breast cancer.

The American Cancer Society was founded in 1913, yet most people have no idea what visual symbol the society uses.

That's the difference between designing a trademark and designing a visual hammer. Almost every brand has a trademark, but few brands have visual hammers.

For his foundation to raise money for cancer research, Lance Armstrong did something similar to Susan G. Komen's pink ribbon.

Amstrong's yellow silicone-gel "Livestrong" bracelet was launched in May 2004 as a fund-raising device. Sold for one dollar each,

more than 70-million Livestrong bracelets have been bought to date.

Today, of course, the Livestrong program is in limbo because of Lance Armstrong's doping confessions.

Too bad, but that is the risk of using a celebrity like Tiger Woods, Bill Cosby or Lance Armstrong in a marketing program.

Pink ribbons, yellow bracelets and other visuals are transforming the nonprofit world. But their successes are based on techniques first developed by the business world.

In 2014, Coca-Cola invested more than $200 million in the U.S. advertising its Coca-Cola brand.

What was Coke's slogan?

Was it "Always?" Or "Enjoy?"

Or perhaps "Coke is it?"

Most people can't remember.

What do most people remember?

What do 99 percent of the American public remember about the advertising of Coca-Cola? Not the words.

Most people remember the "contour" bottle.

The Coca-Cola bottle is not just a bottle. It is a visual hammer that nails in the idea that Coke is the original cola, the authentic cola, the real thing. In a Coca-Cola commercial, the visuals speaks louder than the words. That's the work of a visual hammer.

If you've noticed Coca-Cola advertising in the past few years, you've probably seen a much greater use of its iconic bottle.

In print and television advertising, on the cans, on the packaging and on the billboards. Even on letterheads and calling cards.

The company's visual hammer is one of the reasons why Coca-Cola is the world's third most-valuable brand, worth $79 billion, according to Interbrand, a global branding consultancy.

In today's global economy, a strong visual hammer is a particularly valuable asset. Coca-Cola is sold in 206 countries and 74 percent of the company's revenues come from outside the United States.

In many categories, global brands dominate local brands.

In household and consumer products, global brands have 70 percent of the market in Brazil, 75 percent in China and 90 percent in Russia.

Unlike a verbal concept, a visual hammer can cross global borders with no translations necessary.

What is surprising about Coca-Cola's 6.5-oz. "contour" glass bottle is how few of them are actually bought. No matter. The Coke contour bottle is a powerful visual hammer. A Coke can, on the other hand, is just another can of cola.

That's why it was a smart idea to print the contour bottle on the cans and even on the plastic cups.

One place where the contour bottle is used quite extensively is in high-end restaurants, a fact that speaks to the visual impact the contour bottle has with Coca-Cola customers.

While Coca-Cola has consistently used the same visual hammer, its verbal nails have been repeatedly changed. In the last 110 years, Coke has used 57 different advertising slogans. Most of these are totally forgettable like the 1941 slogan, "Coca-Cola is Coke!"

But four of these advertising slogans could have become long-lasting verbal nails if they had been used continuously.

> 1922:
> **Thirst knows no season.**
> 1929:
> **The pause that refreshes.**
> 1963:
> **Things go better with Coke.**
> 1969:
> **It's the real thing.**

"The real thing," in particular, is a strong verbal nail because it ties in well with the visual hammer. The bottle symbolizes the authenticity of the brand and "the real thing" verbalizes that authenticity. None of the other three slogans, as good as they are, strongly connect to the brand's visual hammer.

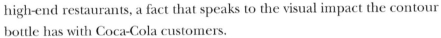

Today, "The real thing" lives on in newspapers, magazines, books and television shows in spite of the fact that the Coca-Cola Company has used the slogan just once, for just two years, more than 40 years ago.

That demonstrates the verbal potency of the idea. It also proves that verbal ideas can get stronger as the years roll by, a reason for keeping a slogan alive for decades.

Yet, most American companies do the opposite. They keep changing their slogans every few years. It's the unintended consequences of the annual slew of "creativity" awards.

You can't be a successful advertising agency today unless you can win your share of awards. And you can't win an advertising award if you used last year's slogan. It's not "creative." That is, it's not new and different.

So advertising agencies face a difficult choice. Win awards or perish. You can't blame them for choosing the former.

Coca-Cola's exceptionally-strong visual hammer puts its major competitor in a difficult position. What should Pepsi-Cola do?

The management at PepsiCo, like many other executives, seems to think that a visual hammer is nothing but a glorified name for a trademark. That's why they tend to spend a lot of time and money  perfecting their trademarks rather than creating visual hammers.

Back in 2008, PepsiCo said it would invest more than $1.2 billion over the next three years revamping, according to CEO Indra Nooyi, "every aspect of the brand proposition for our key brands."

"How they look, how they're packaged, how they are merchandised on the shelves and how they connect with consumers."

As part of that revamping, Pepsi-Cola has a new trademark and a new advertising campaign which in a recent year the company spent $225 million promoting.

So how many consumers know Pepsi's new slogan?

Not many.

A trademark is not a visual hammer. If the "contour" bottle

"Refresh everything."

Old.   New.

says "the original, authentic cola," what does Pepsi's new trademark say?

Pepsi's new "smiley-face" mark says "Pepsi." In essence, it's a rebus, a visual symbol that is a substitute for a brand name.

Almost all trademarks are rebuses. After many years of constant use (and millions of advertising dollars), they are perceived as visual symbols that stand for brand names.

But trademarks generally don't communicate much more than that.

And many trademarks don't even do that. Do you recognize these two trademarks? Reebok's old trademark is on the left and its new trademark on the right.

Does your brand have a visual hammer? Or does it have a meaningless, rebus trademark? Or perhaps it has no visual at all.

Not all trademarks are meaningless. Nike has the Swoosh, a powerful visual hammer. What's the difference between the Reebok logos and the Nike Swoosh? The Swoosh doesn't just say "Nike."

The Swoosh also says "leadership."

The trademark on Tiger's cap hammers Nike's leadership position into consumers' mind. And it's not because the Swoosh is in any way special. Nike could have taken any simple and unique visual and over time its visual could have become a powerful hammer.

What gave Nike the ability to create a visual hammer out of a rather ordinary symbol? (A checkmark that has been streamlined.)

Being first in a new category.

Nike was the first athletic-shoe brand. And today, Nike dominates the athletic-shoe category.

A visual hammer doesn't just repeat your brand name; it hammers a specific word into the mind. For brands that can create and dominate a new category, that word is "leadership."

Simplicity is the key when creating a visual hammer like the Swoosh.

Too many trademark designers think they are designing a coat of arms for some mythical 15th century warrior rather than a symbol for a 21st century company.

Simplicity combined with uniqueness allows a visual hammer to be instantly recognizable.

The original Mercedes-Benz trademark had a lot of pomp but very little power.

Trademarks shouldn't be thought of as mere decorations.

For market leaders in particular, trademarks are potential visual hammers like the Mercedes mark.

The new Mercedes trademark represents the ultimate in simplicity. Today, the Tri-Star symbol is one of the strongest visual hammers in the world. As the original "prestige" automobile, the Tri-Star hammers the word "prestige" into the automobile buyer's mind.

Brands that create new categories have a singular opportunity to create a visual hammer that represents leadership and authenticity. But not every brand gets it right.

Take Red Bull, for example. The company was first in the energy-drink category which Red Bull dominates with annual global sales of $6.7 billion.

Despite its success, Red Bull doesn't own a visual hammer in minds. It had the opportunity, but the visual it chose is much too complicated for a small 8.3-oz. energy-drink can.

"Two bulls and a sun" make a weak hammer. It doesn't measure up to the power of the Tri-Star, the Swoosh or the Coke bottle. (It doesn't make sense to use two bulls as a visual when the verbal has only one.)

If the leader lacks a potent visual hammer, it gives the No. 2 brand a golden opportunity. Monster entered the energy-drink market by positioning itself as the opposite of Red Bull.

Monster was launched with a 16-oz. can as compared with Red Bull's 8.3-oz. can. The oversize can and the Monster brand name link well together in consumers' minds.

Monster also made a good visual choice. Claw marks in the shape of an "M" send a subtle message of "strength" and "danger" in an effective way.

As a result, you remember the Monster visual hammer.

Today, Monster is a strong No. 2 brand with 37 percent of the energy-drink market (Red Bull has 45 percent), in part because of the use of its "claw marks" visual hammer at concerts and sporting events.

In spite of these and many other examples, why are many marketers working exclusively with words, when the real power is with visuals?

Well, words are important, too.

The Ultimate
Driving Machine

2

NAIL

THE ULTIMATE OBJECTIVE.

Since a visual has more emotional impact than a verbal, it's logical to assume that the first decision a marketer needs to make is what visual to use in its marketing program.

Not so.

That's a paradox that is bound to confuse many marketing people. While a visual hammer can be effective in building a brand, that's not the objective of a marketing program. The objective of a marketing program is to "own a word in the mind."

BMW, for example, owns the word "driving," an achievement that lifted the brand from nowhere into its position as the world's largest-selling luxury-vehicle brand.

But what put the "driving" idea into the minds of consumers?

It was BMW's visual hammer. A long-running series of television commercials showing happy owners driving BMWs over winding roads.

"The ultimate driving machine" was the nail. But it was the visual hammer was put the "driving" nail into the mind.

Without the hammer, in my opinion, the verbal idea would have been road kill. After all, "driving" has been a consistent theme of auto advertising for many decades, including "We build excitement," a long-running Pontiac campaign without a visual hammer.

But if the objective is to own a word in the mind, why fool around with a visual hammer? Why not just focus your brand's entire marketing effort on a verbal approach?

Consider a nail and a hammer. If the objective is to nail two pieces of wood together, why fool around with a hammer? Why not focus all your efforts on putting the two pieces of wood together with a nail?

That's the essential problem of marketing. Your most important tool is a hammer which is redundant once you have nailed your positioning idea into prospects' minds.

Well, not exactly. The three rules of advertising are: (1) Repetition, (2) Repetition, and (3) Repetition.

So you need to hammer away, not just for years, but for decades. And not just in your advertising but in everything you do from websites to business cards to annual reports.

"The ultimate driving machine" campaign was launched in 1975. By 1993, BMW was the largest-selling imported European luxury vehicle.

In the 18 years since, BMW has outsold the No.2 brand (Mercedes) 14 of those 18 years.

So what did BMW do recently? They switched their focus to "joy" and you can understand why.

Joy is a unique verbal concept that broadens the appeal of the BMW brand. Which is true but how do you visualize it?

Like many high-level abstract

JOY IS IN GOOD COMPANY.

JOY IS THE NEW BMW 3 SERIES
COUPE AND CONVERTIBLE.

words (happiness, customer satisfaction, product quality) joy cannot be visualized in any meaningful way. As a result, BMW has paid the price for its excursion into "joy."

In the past five years, from 2010 to 2014, BMW has fallen to second place behind its long-time rival, Mercedes-Benz.

Many marketing slogans are ineffective for one simple reason. They might express an important benefit of the brand, but unless they can be reinforced by a visual hammer, they are useless.

What do consumers look for when they buy an automobile? Among other things, they look for: reliability, good gas mileage, good looks, nice interiors, drivability and the right size.

The first mistake automobile manufacturers make is to advertise all these features. That's logical. That's what consumers want.

Big mistake. When you advertise everything, your prospects remember nothing.

The second mistake is to pick your brand's most important feature. But that only works if that feature can be turned into a visual hammer.

Take Volvo, for example. Years ago, the company latched onto "safety" as its verbal nail, and then hammered that idea with dramatic TV commercials featuring crash tests.

WE DESIGN EVERY VOLVO TO LOOK LIKE THIS.

Every year in the 23 years from 1970 to 1992 (except for the single year 1977), Volvo was the largest-selling European luxury-vehicle brand in the American market.

In those 22 years, Volvo outsold BMW, Mercedes, Audi and Jaguar. Then in 1993, things started to fall apart.

In the last two decades, Volvo has driven away from its safety focus. Gone are the crash tests. Even the slogan was weak: "Volvo. For life."

In order to increase sales, Volvo even tried to promote performance. Volvo introduced sports cars, even Volvo convertibles.

As Volvo's director of global advertising once said: "Safety on its own is not enough."

That's left-brain thinking.

Volvo convertible.

Logic suggests consumers don't buy cars just because they're safe. They look for a lot of other things before they buy a vehicle.

But unless a vehicle brand gets into the consumer's mind and unless the consumer gets into a dealer's showroom, logical thinking is useless.

In marketing, everything else is secondary to the job of getting into consumers' minds. And without a powerful visual hammer, that job is exceedingly difficult to do.

Volvo continues to drift downward. From a high of 113,267 vehicles in 1986, Volvo sold just 56,366 vehicles in 2014. That year, both BMW and Mercedes-Benz sold more than six times as many vehicles as Volvo. Even Audi sold more than three times as many vehicles as Volvo.

Volvo's biggest mistake was to abandon a successful visual hammer. And after it did that, the brand suffered.

Over the long term, a consistent visual hammer is more important than a consistent verbal nail, although it's better to have both.

Consider the Marlboro cowboy, perhaps an even more-effective visual hammer than the Coca-Cola contour bottle. Introduced in 1953, the cowboy turned Marlboro into the world's best-selling cigarette.

(The brand's share of the American market is 43 percent, more than the next 13 cigarette brands combined.)

Since its initial launch 62 years ago, Marlboro has never run an ad, a commercial or an in-store promotion without using cowboy imagery. Nor has Marlboro ever used a woman in its "cowboy" advertising.

(Actually, since its "re-launch," as Marlboro was once a woman's cigarette, but that's another story.)

Many brands have tried to copy the success of the Marlboro cowboy. Pick up a magazine, look at a newspaper, turn on your television set, surf the Internet, and you'll find hundreds of visuals that try to mimic the success of the cowboy.

Monkeys, donkeys, dogs, frogs, elephants, kids, babies, sexy women, older women, sexy older women, hot men, older men, hot older men, celebrities and many other visuals.

Most of these visuals never become hammers. Why is this?

Because art directors select visuals that are funny, serious, cute, sexy, or famous without first considering what the verbal ought to be.

You need two things to build a brand. A visual hammer and a verbal nail. And the nail comes first.

At the time of Marlboro's introduction, the majority of competitive brands were "unisex." Cigarette brands that made the classic mistake of appealing to everybody.

Marlboro was the first masculine cigarette. That's the verbal nail. And what could be more masculine than a cowboy? (Not much, in my opinion as an avid spectator of professional bull-riding.)

Most brand visuals never become hammers. They might be funny, but unless they are also functional they will do little for the brand.

A good example are the frogs from the 1995 Budweiser Super Bowl commercial, often listed as one of the best in TV history.

The television commercial shows a swamp at nighttime with three frogs rhythmically croaking "Bud"... "Weis"... "Er."

Brilliant, right? I don't think so. Three frogs croaking "Budweiser." Where's the verbal nail?

Frogs, dogs, lizards. Budweiser has used all these animals and more. All the while, the brand has the ultimate visual hammer which it uses only occasionally.

That visual is the Clydesdale horses pulling an old-fashioned beer wagon. They hammer in the authenticity of the brand, the King of Beers. The horses also say "old," which is a good thing in beverages.

In technology, it's good to be new. In beverages, it's better to be old. Witness the success of brands like Dom Perignon founded in 1693.

Instead of sticking with the visual it already owns (the Clydesdales) as well as its companion verbal nail (King of Beers), Budweiser keeps searching for a new idea.

The latest is "Here we go." Before that it was "Drinkability." Both of these verbal ideas are almost impossible to visualize.

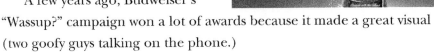

A few years ago, Budweiser's "Wassup?" campaign won a lot of awards because it made a great visual (two goofy guys talking on the phone.)

But as a verbal idea it lacked motivation. What does "Wassup" have to do with drinking Budweiser beer?

Logical managers tend to prefer ideas that encompass everything. Like Chevrolet's latest slogan "Find new roads."

Even if Chevrolet manages to put the idea into the mind, where's the motivation to buy a Chevrolet vehicle?

Then too, when your idea is a high-level abstraction or a concept

that is broad and general, it's almost impossible to find a visual hammer that will drive the idea into prospects' minds.

Effective visual hammers need narrow nails like driving and safety. (Real hammers need narrow nails, too.)

How can anyone find a visual hammer that symbolizes democracy, loyalty, trust and other high-level abstractions?

Consumers tend to take verbal ideas like "Find new roads" literally. It sounds like an advertising slogan for Range Rover, whose owners often get off the main roads to explore the back country.

Abstract ideas needs to be brought down to earth before they can be turned into visual hammers.

3

SHAPE

SIMPLE IS BETTER.

Suppose you were put in charge of marketing an organization that called itself, "International Committee for Relief to the Wounded."

What visual hammer would you use?

None of the organization's words (international, committee, relief and wounded) can be visualized in a unique way. Fortunately, five years after its founding, the organization changed its name to "International Committee for the Red Cross," which is still its official designation today.

With 97 million volunteers, supporters and office staff in 186 countries, the Red Cross is one of the world's largest nonprofit organizations.

American Red Cross

(The American Red Cross is an independent organization that works closely with the International Committee for the Red Cross.)

When you are searching for a visual hammer, you start with the nail. But here's the paradox. Often you have to sacrifice something.

"Relief to the Wounded" is more meaningful than "Red Cross." No matter. Relief and Wounded can't be visualized in a simple way while Red Cross can.

The ultimate objective of a marketing program is to hammer an idea into the prospect's mind. But sometimes it's much easier to hitchhike on an idea that's already there.

The Red Cross has made the word and the color "red" synonymous with a nonprofit charity organization. So U2 lead-singer Bono and Bobby Shriver (son of Sargent Shriver) created Product Red to raise money to fight AIDS in Africa.

The Product Red brand is licensed to partner companies like Apple, Converse, Dell, Gap, Hallmark, Nike and Starbucks. Each company creates a product with the Product Red logo and a percentage of the company's profits is given to the Global Fund to Fight AIDS, Tuberculosis and Malaria.

Product Red is the largest private-sector donor to the Global Fund and has generated over $200 million for AIDS programs in Africa.

It's interesting that the Red Cross and Product Red are well known, but the Global Fund to Fight AIDS, Tuberculosis and Malaria is not.

Where is the visual hammer for the Global Fund? It needs a name change to make one possible. In other words, you sometimes need to sharpen your verbal nail before searching for a visual hammer.

As far as shapes are concerned, there are only a handful of unique shapes most people can recognize.

Furthermore, most common shapes (the sun, the star, the rectangle, the circle, the arrow, the triangle, the checkmark) are used by so many brands that they have become virtually useless as visuals hammers.

Adding a unique color can help, but even many color and shape combinations have been pre-empted.

The Red Star, for example, by both Russia and China.

Simplicity should be your guiding principle when looking for a potential visual hammer. It's not a coincidence that three of the world's major religions all use symbols that are extremely simple.

The Star & Crescent, the Cross and the Star of David.

Many of the simpler shapes are already taken by existing brands. The "target," for example, is used by both the detergent and the stores.

Tide's "target" hammer works exceptionally well because Tide was the first brand in a new category.

It also helps that the name "Tide" looks like it's stuck in the center of the target logotype.

As far as the "target" of the Target stores is concerned, the utter simplicity of this design is what gives the trademark its power.

It may not be aesthetically pleasing, but in the retail category Target's "target" is undoubtedly the most distinctive and most memorable trademark in the field.

Compare Target's target with Walmart's new symbol, a six-petal design that resembles a flower.

Some reporters have speculated that the new symbol reflects former chief executive H. Lee Scott's goal of transforming Walmart into an environmentally-friendly company.

If so, the symbol does neither that job nor does the sunflower serve as an effective visual hammer. Too bad.

Walmart is the largest retailer in the world, the dominant brand in the mass-merchandiser category. It should have been relatively easy for Walmart to develop a distinctive visual hammer.

The company's first try, a star that also served as a hypen in the Walmart name, was banality at its best. The sunflower is a close second.

The trademark world is loaded with circles, squares, stars, arrows and other conventional shapes. Almost all of these shapes are useless in the process of creating a visual hammer.

A much better approach is to try to create a unique new shape.

One that has become well known around the world is the "peace" symbol, designed in 1958.

The peace symbol is unique, but it shares some similarities with Mercedes' Tri-Star trademark.

Recently, Under Armour created a unique new visual hammer that has also become relatively well known.

Although simple, it's actually more complicated than it needs to be. At a distance, the mark looks like an "H" in spite of the fact designers

tried to create a symbolic "UA" for the Under Armour name.

In evaluating trademarks, one mistake marketing people often make is asking questions like: "Do we like the design?"

"Is there anyway we can improve the way our trademark design looks?"

What a trademark looks like is immaterial. A more appropriate question to ask is: "What message does the trademark communicate to customers and prospects?"

The object of a visual hammer is to hammer a word in the mind. In Under Armour's case it is "Leadership in moisture-wicking garments designed to be worn under sports uniforms."

No visual can communicate the moisture-wicking idea so it needs to be done symbolically. Luckily, the "UA" in the Under Armour trademark is not obvious to most consumers.

If it were, the Under Armour mark would lose some of its value as a "moisture-wicking" visual hammer.

Many companies use initials as a trademark. "A" for Ally Bank. "HP" for Hewlett-Packard. "GE" for General Electric.

In effect, initials like "hp" are just shorthand symbols for the brand names themselves.

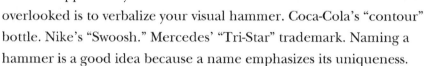

They don't hammer in any unique verbal idea.

One opportunity that is often overlooked is to verbalize your visual hammer. Coca-Cola's "contour" bottle. Nike's "Swoosh." Mercedes' "Tri-Star" trademark. Naming a hammer is a good idea because a name emphasizes its uniqueness.

McDonald's uses an initial "M" as a trademark. But by naming the symbol, "the Golden Arches," the company moved beyond the rebus idea and turned the "M" into an effective visual hammer.

Golden Arches visualizes the company's leadership in fast food.

Unlike what the art community might be telling you, visuals never work their way into human minds totally on their own. To be filed away in the mind, a visual needs to be verbalized. Art critics, for example, will file this picture under "Cubism." Then under "Picasso." And if they are real experts under a subfile "Women of d'Avignon."

Artwork has no meaning until it is verbalized.

Watch art lovers stroll through a museum. If they don't recognize a painting, they will look at the bottom of the art to read the name of the artist who painted it.

(Without a name, a piece of artwork is not worth very much.)

A good visual hammer takes advantage of this phenomenon. To judge the effectiveness of a hammer, you have to constantly ask, What is this potential hammer saying?

Because they create an emotional response, two strong visual shapes are the phallic symbol, associated with the male sexual organ, and the kirkos symbol, associated with the female sexual organ.

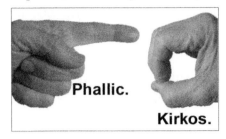

Phallic.

Kirkos.

Visuals using either of these shapes can make very effective hammers. Two examples are:

The contour bottle, a phallic symbol, and the Tri-Star, a kirkos symbol.

The weakest shape is the square.

Why in the world would H&R Block, the leading income-tax service, use a green square as its visual?

Presumably, management thought, Our name is Block and a block is a square.

H&R BLOCK

So we'll use a square to remind people of our name and we'll make it green, the color of money. But consumers don't see it that way. They don't see a "block." They see a dull, green, empty square.

Look at how many people use "shapes" in the vernacular. A "square" is somebody who is "not with it."

On the other hand, the word "circle" is usually used in a positive way. As the social-media site says: "Google+ lets users organize people into Circles of friends."

Neat, organized, buttoned-down people (typically left brainers) often use squares or rectangles for symbols because they reflect their "don't-rock-the-boat" outlook on life. But if you want to call attention to a symbol, you should avoid dullness at all costs.

Take The Gap. The clothing chain's logotype is a blue square with the letters "GAP" in white type.

Not particularly eye-catching, so it was understandable why the chain wanted a new logotype.

But the revise was terrible. Instead of moving away from a dull, blue square, the designer emphasized the square by using it assymetrically.

What in the world was the redesign of The Gap logo trying to do? Symbolize blue jeans for squares?

After unveiling The Gap's new assymetrical logo in October 2010, the company received a barrage of negative feedback from customers.

The Internet was literally ablaze with the backlash. So the old Gap logo was promptly brought back.

What should The Gap do? Since consumers "verbalize the visual," one way to approach the problem is to "visualize the verbal."

The Gap's long-term advertising slogan was: "Fall into the Gap." Instead of a free-floating square, why didn't The Gap try to visualize the "fall into" idea?

Perhaps by using a symbolic funnel or something similar that could hammer the "fall into" nail into the mind of the consumer.

J.C.Penney also followed in the footsteps of The Gap, moving from a square to a typographic logotype with a smaller decorative square.

I'm amazed that hordes of Penney customers didn't complain about the new logotype.

In addition to a dull square, why would J.C.Penney split its name in half, so it reads: "JCP/enny?"

Furthermore, Kentucky Fried Chicken was often called "KFC," so that name change made some

sense. But J.C.Penney was never called "JCP." So why use initials?

While the new J.C.Penney logotype was undeniably more attractive than the previous one, attractiveness is not the most important criteria in designing a logotype.

That's the problem with the Gatorade logotype. The lightning bolt is so attractive it doesn't look like a lightning bolt anymore.

It looks more like a knife than a lightning bolt. But it gets worse.

The name disappears on the new Gatorade logo to be replaced by the letter "G." That's a mistake. Who calls Gatorade by its initial letter? "Give me a G" won't get you a Gatorade in any store.

Old.   New.

Sometimes a brand's nickname is used so often that companies are forced to include it on the labels.

The Coca-Cola Company, for example, added the word "Coke" on its beverage cans. But note: Coca-Cola didn't label the brand "CC," because nobody called its cola brand CC.

How badly will the "G" logotype change hurt the Gatorade brand? In the short term, not at all. But long term, there are problems.

Marketing is essentially a long-term discipline. Marketing is more like a tree farm than a vegetable garden. In the long term, the Gatorade brand is bound to suffer.

Consider the fact that worldwide 490,000 babies are born each day. That's almost half-a-million potential Gatorade consumers who will have to learn to associate the "G" with the Gatorade name.

Why doesn't the company make the process easier by keeping the Gatorade name on its logotype?

Furthermore, some 275,000 people die every day. Many of these are loyal Gatorade customers who take their knowledge of what "G" means to the grave with them.

4

COLOR

BE THE OPPOSITE.

Color can be an effective visual hammer, but there's a problem. There are few distinct colors in the spectrum. Five primary colors: Blue, green, yellow, orange and red. And a few secondary ones.

If you happen to get in early, you can enhance the reputation of your brand by pre-empting a specific color. Tiffany, for example, has pre-empted the color blue.

Introduced in 1878, Tiffany "blue" has become a worldwide icon for the high-end jewelry store.

As a visual hammer, "blue" communicates the elegance and authenticity of the Tiffany brand.

The color is a private Pantone custom color and is even legally protected as a color trademark. Tiffany stores have one thing in stock that you cannot buy. They will only give it to you. The blue box.

The rule of the establishment is ironclad, never to allow a box bearing the name of the firm to be taken out of the building except with an article sold by them and for which they are responsible.

The Tiffany box is a very effective visual hammer. Put a blue box on a table and a white box from some other jewelry store next to it and watch the reaction of a typical woman. The blue box will generate an emotional reaction and the other box will not.

Kodak did the same with "yellow." The yellow box communicates Kodak's leadership in photographic film. A green box of Fujifilm just isn't the same. Unless it's a lot cheaper, or the store doesn't have Kodak in stock, most consumers won't buy "green" when they can get "yellow."

But note: A hammer is useless without a nail. The yellow box hammers Kodak's photographic-film leadership. But photographic film is practically dead today because photography has gone digital.

So Kodak made the classic error of trying to use its Kodak name and its yellow hammer on a line of digital products. The results have been quite dismal. In the decade of the 1990's (from 1991 to 2000 when photographic film still reigned supreme), Kodak had sales of $125.2 billion and net profits after taxes of $6.9 billion, or a net profit margin of 4.5 percent. In the following decade (from 2001 to 2010), Kodak had sales of $115.0 billion and lost $917 million.

No wonder the Kodak company went bankrupt in 2012.

Compare Kodak's results with Shutterfly, a small company with a single focus (digital prints via the web) and a single color (orange.)

In the last ten years, Shutterfly had revenues of $3.1 billion and net profits of $122 million.

Kodak tried to compete with Shutterfly using a website called Kodak Gallery. Another example of the folly of line extension.

Why didn't Kodak give its Kodak Gallery website a different name?

(In a big company, "loyalty" is the ultimate virtue. The principles of marketing are not something managers pay attention to when the principles conflict with their loyalties to their companies.)

What should Kodak have done? It should have launched a digital line with a different name.

Failing that, it would have been helpful to launch a digital line with a different color to differentiate Kodak's new digital products from its older photographic-film products.

Much like Ralph Lauren did when it launched its highest-priced men's line as "Ralph Lauren Purple Label."

The Red Cross is one of the most famous charity organizations in the world. So back in 1929, a Baylor University executive developed a hospital plan which he called "Blue Cross." Ten years later, another organization was formed called "Blue Shield."

Blue Cross and Blue Shield developed separately, with Blue Cross plans providing coverage for hospital services, while Blue Shield plans covered physician services. Eventually, the two organizations merged.

Today, the combined Blue Cross/Blue Shield Association is a federation of 39 separate health insurance organizations and companies in America.

Combined, they directly or indirectly provide health insurance to over 100 million Americans.

"Blue" is the color that differentiates the Blue Cross/Blue Shield brand. The confusion factor is the fact that the two names and symbols are used together. (Either one would have made an effective verbal and visual strategy for the association.)

In too many mergers, marketing effectiveness takes a backseat to corporate ego. As a result, executives try to please both organizations.

Sometimes you can take a simple product, but paint it an unusual color and create an effective visual hammer.

In 1968, Mary Kay Ash purchased a Cadillac and had it painted pink
to promote her line of cosmetics.

The car was such a terrific
advertisement for the Mary Kay
brand that the following year
she rewarded her top five
producers with pink Cadillacs.

Today, Mary Kay is a global firm with annual sales of $2.5 billion.
More than two-million independent consultants demonstrate Mary Kay
products in the U.S. and some 35 other countries. Consultants vie for
awards each year, ranging from jewelry to pink Cadillacs.

General Motors estimates that it has built 100,000 pink Cadillacs for
Mary Kay to give to her top producers.

How do you tell one Caribbean island from another? They all have

sand, sea, surf, palm trees and
overpriced hotels. Bermuda
found a way. Pink sand.

(And Bermuda is not even
an island in the Caribbean!)

Is pink sand any better than
tan or beige or white sand? No, but it's different and that's always the
first thing to look for when you're looking for a visual hammer.

One thing Bermuda doesn't do is to connect its unique pink-sand
hammer to a memorable verbal nail.

Instead it uses a cliché that could apply to almost any island or any
brand. "So much more."

In the professional golf world, there are four major championships:
(1) The U.S. Open, (2) The British Open, (3) The PGA Championship
and (4) The Masters.

The first three are hosted by major golf organizations, but the
Masters is hosted by a private club, the Augusta National Golf Club.

Which golf tournament draws the most attention? The Masters in
Augusta, Georgia, of course.

One reason is the green jacket, the symbol of a Masters Champion dating back to the year 1937.

That year, members of the Augusta club wore green jackets during the tournament so fans in attendance could easily spot them if they wanted to ask questions.

Visual symbols are not only memorable, but they also tend to elevate the importance of the event or the person who wears the symbol.

When a leader of the Catholic Church is promoted to Cardinal, what picture is published around the world?

The new Cardinal in his red hat, of course.

(Cardinals of the Catholic Church wear red hats, it is said, because the red hat is a symbol that they are ready to shed their blood to defend their faith, a nice verbal nail.)

For years, the real-estate-firm Century 21 insisted its agents wear gold jackets. You might be surprised at how many Century 21 agents objected to wearing a "uniform."

Yet the gold jacket was probably the best marketing idea Century 21 has ever developed.

Century 21 sometimes uses the verbal nail, "The Gold Standard."

But the verbal nail might be stronger if Century 21 used it consistently and if they had qualified their verbal nail by saying, "The Gold Standard in Real Estate."

Then there's Christian Louboutin, a French designer who regularly tops The Luxury Institute's index of "most prestigious women's shoes."

In 1992, he applied red nail polish to the sole of a shoe because he felt the shoes lacked energy.

"This was such a success," reported Mr. Louboutin, "that it became a permanent fixture."

The red sole was the visual hammer, but what was the verbal nail?

It was the stiletto (heel heights of 120mm or more) which Christian Louboutin helped bring back into fashion in the last two decades.

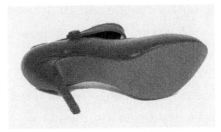

To build a brand you need both: The red sole and the stiletto.

A color hammer can be particularly effective in the retail field. It's hard to miss a McDonald's, even driving down the road at 50 miles an hour. On America's highways, those golden arches are a magnet.

Waffle House also has a visual magnet to capture the traveling motorist. Giant yellow letters that spell out its brand name.

Many Waffle House units take the idea one step further. They use giant yellow awnings to reinforce the brand's identity.

What might the next step be? Paint the entire building yellow. This might be a good direction for Waffle House and almost any other brand associated with a single color.

Red Roof Inn is a motel brand using red roofs as a color identifier and a visual hammer. What's missing is a verbal nail that would connect the red roof to some consumer benefit.

When it comes to color, many retailers miss the paint bucket.

Many retailers tend to design their signage for attractiveness rather than for uniqueness.

Look at Exxon, one of the world's largest gas-station chains. Hertz is yellow, Starbucks is green, Avis is red, Tiffany is blue, but what color is Exxon?

Exxon red-and-blue gas stations are not nearly as visible on roads and highways as single-color gasoline stations like "yellow" Shell locations. Or "green" BP stations.

The air-cargo-carrier Federal Express got off the ground with a verbal nail: "When it absolutely, positively, has to be there overnight." But what was the visual hammer for the FedEx brand?

The overnight letter, of course. When a Federal Express envelope arrived, the company wanted to make sure it received the maximum amount of attention from the recipient. So Federal Express picked  the two colors most likely to stand out in a dull office environment.

Purple and orange.

An excellent choice for Federal Express in the short term because the two colors were shocking, but not in the long term where a single color might have been better.

Then FedEx, the new name for the company, did what most companies do. After expanding into many other services, Fedex uses color to differentiate them.

Red for "express." Blue for "custom critical." Green for "ground."

Today, FedEx is a rainbow company, associated with no particular color. That's a typical pattern many companies follow.

Its major competitor, United Parcel Service, took a different approach. Instead of using one of the colors you see everywhere, UPS selected "brown," one of the least-popular colors.

(Most companies are focused on being "better" when the real opportunity lies in being "different." Even in color.)

Today, brown is as strongly identified with UPS as blue is with Tiffany. So strong, in fact, the company runs advertisements with the headline, "What can Brown do for you?"

Brown is a strong visual hammer, but the current UPS nail is weak. "We love logistics."

I love consulting, too, but "I love consulting" wouldn't make a good verbal nail for our marketing- strategy firm.

It's much too generic.

What would make a good verbal nail for a Brown visual hammer? Almost every good verbal nail is competitive in nature. It differentiates the brand from its major competitors.

What differentiates UPS from FedEx? Not logistics, a discipline that both companies practice.

"Leadership" is one possibility, but I think there is a much bigger opportunity for UPS. As shopping moves from physical to Internet stores, UPS could borrow an idea

from the yellow pages and position itself as the ideal shipping service for today's digital customers.

Everybody knows the Starbucks logotype is green, but what color is its competitor, Dunkin' Donuts?

There are more than 6,700 Dunkin' Donuts locations in America, almost all of them east of the Mississippi river. But most people don't associate the coffee brand with any particular color. Dunkin' Donuts' orange-and-pink signage is attractive but not nearly as memorable as the green mermaid at Starbucks or the yellow "M" at McDonald's.

Have you ever wondered why most beer bottles are "brown?"

Actually, almost all beer bottles were green in color until the 1930s when it was discovered that brown bottles filtered out the light that caused beer to go "skunky."

(Sunlight breaks down acids in hops that react with sulfur to produce a chemical nearly identical to one that skunks spray. Gives new meaning to the toast "bottoms up.")

In Europe after World War II, there was a shortage of brown glass, so many brewers of beer including Heineken exported their beer in green bottles.

As the leading imported beer in America, Heineken became closely associated with the color "green."

Trade papers called Heineken "The Green Standard." Beer drinkers asked for a "greenie."

Today, the green bottle and the green label are a visual hammer for the Heineken brand. But what is Heineken's verbal nail?

Over the years, Heineken has explored ideas like: "Seek the truth." And: "It's all true." And: "It's all about the beer." And: "Satisfy your thirst for the best." And the latest slogan: "Open your world." There's also the U.K. slogan: "Refreshes the parts other beers cannot reach."

These are all classic mistakes. A leader should generally emphasize its leadership. At one point, Heineken had about 40 percent of the imported beer market, twice the share of Molson, the No.2 brand.

Then Corona from Mexico entered the market with a powerful visual hammer, the lime on top of the bottle. By 1997, Heineken had fallen to second place. Then they did something that made no sense.

They redesigned the Heineken label to enlarge what previously was a tiny red star. Then they built an ad campaign around the idea.

"Stare at this for a long time and you'll see a red star."

Naturally, the beer drinker was confused. "Is this a Russian beer?"

And Heineken fell further behind Corona.

You can change "words" in a marketing program, but heaven help you if you try to change a "visual."

If you succeed in establishing a strong visual hammer (the cowboy, the duck, the lime, the straw-in-the-orange, the red soles and dozens of others), you cannot change your visual hammer without substantially damaging your brand.

So you're stuck with your current visual hammer. But what an effective device it can be for decades to come.

The surprising thing is how few companies show pictures of their visual hammers on the products themselves.

Why doesn't Corona use a lime on its label? And why doesn't Budweiser use the Clydesdales on its label?

Companies spend millions to put visual and verbal ideas into consumers' minds and then don't bother to put them on their labels.

Another remarkable success story in the beer business is Coors Light, the Silver Bullet, now with a 10-percent market share.

(What green did for Heineken, "silver" is doing for Coors Light.)

Thanks to its Silver Bullet, Coors Light has already passed Miller Lite which has fallen to 7.9 percent.

(Massive line extensions have greatly weakened the Miller brand. Starting with Miller High Life, the brand has been extended with Miller regular, Miller Clear, Miller Chill, Miller Genuine Draft, Miller Genuine Draft Light, Lite Ice, Miller Reserve, Miller Reserve Amber Ale, Lite Genuine Draft, Lite Ultra, Miller Genuine Draft 64 and others.)

Still, Coors Light is a long way from Bud Light which currently has a 25-percent market share.

But I predict the Coors Light brand will continue to increase its lead over Miller Lite, thanks to the Silver Bullet. (In 2011, Coors Light passed Budweiser to become the second-largest beer brand.)

Budweiser, the King of Beers, struck back with a unique twist to reinforce its verbal nail.

The new Budweiser cans have a red pull tab with the "crown" symbol embedded in the tab, a visual idea that is hard to miss.

On Budweiser bottles, the brewer has a new cap designed to keep oxygen out and flavor in.

Called "Flavor-lock crown," the new cap uses a visual crown, but it's not the same as the crown used on the red plastic pull tab.

That's a mistake. Consistency in names, slogans and visual hammers is what builds brands. Not variety.

The same is true in color. Single-color brands are usually better than multiple-color brands. Compare Burger King with McDonald's.

While McDonald's restaurants seems to be everywhere, Burger King units are mostly out-of-sight. What color are Burger King signs?

Most Burger King units have massive kids playgrounds. But that's

Old.   **New.**

what McDonald's is known for. So the logotype on the building is the only thing that differentiates a Burger King from a McDonald's.

The old Burger King logo at least looked like a hamburger. The new logo looks like abstract art.

Sometimes the color a brand should use is obvious. Yet some companies even screw this up.

Look at Virgin Blue, an Australian airline that painted

its planes "red." How can Virgin Blue burn the name "Virgin Blue" in the prospect's mind with red airplanes?

Red Bull made the same mistake. While Virgin Blue planes are red, Red Bull cans are primarily blue, except for Red Bull cola which is half red, half blue. (Another line extension that didn't work.)

Often a brand starts off as a single color. Then management decides to line-extend the brand into many different categories as Red Bull did.

So the problem arises, how does the brand differentiate itself between its various categories?

One of the most common ways is by using different colors. In the process, the brand's original color is lost.

When it comes to color, retailers should not just try to associate a logotype with a single color. Retailers should try to associate the entire store with a single color.

Years ago, Elizabeth Arden painted the front door of its New York retail salon "red."

The "red door" has become a trademark for the Elizabeth Arden brand, currently used on 31 Red Door spas and also its line of Elizabeth Arden Red Door spa products.

Almost every newspaper in the world is printed on grey newsprint, except for the Financial Times which is printed on salmon-colored stock. In an era where newspapers have been losing money, the Financial Times is profitable with about 2 million readers.

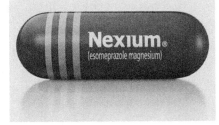

It took a bit of courage for AstraZenica to introduce Nexium, a heartburn-relief pharmaceutical drug, in a purple pill.

At one point, Nexium the purple pill was the second-largest prescription drug in dollar sales in the American market.

AstraZenica, the maker of Nexium, even runs a website called (naturally) PurplePill.com.

Red is the color that demands the most attention. As in stop signs. Something unusual is often called a "red flag" even though it has nothing to do with color or flags.

That's why red is the most-often-used retail color outside the stores. Inside the stores, it's a different matter. Inside the stores, retailers prefer laid-back colors like greens and blues to encourage consumers to focus on the products and not on the stores' décor.

Enter Redbox, the big, garish, red-colored DVD-rental kiosks that are revolutionizing the industry.

Inside a supermarket, they are hard to miss and their $1-a-night rental price is hard to resist.

While Blockbuster filed for bankruptcy in 2010, Redbox's owner, Coinstar, has been consistently profitable. Annual Redbox sales are approximately $1 billion.

Many old established brands like MasterCard and Visa use multiple colors. They were designed to look good, but not necessarily to stand out from the crowd.

That's a disadvantage in today's crowded marketplace.

What colors do MasterCard and Visa use? You probably don't remember. These are two of the many examples of the folly of multiple-color brands.

Steven Streit had an idea to compete with the established credit-card companies. His idea was a prepaid debit card for people without a bank account or access to credit. What color should such a card use?

When you are first in a new category, forget expensive designers and artistic taste. The obvious color is green, the color of money. And what is the simplest symbol you can use for a visual?

A circle, obviously. So the name became Green Dot, the first prepaid debit card and a big success.

In seven years of operations, sales have grown to $574 million annually with $34 million in net profits. Green Dot's recent market cap was a hefty $833 million.

Look at the success of the Keurig Green Mountain company. Thanks to the increasing use of single-serve K-Cups, the Green Mountain brand has grown very rapidly.

Sales in 2004 were $137 million.

Ten years later, sales had jumped to $4.7 billion.

Sometimes you can also be successful by picking a color that is functionally less effective.

Look what an effective hammer the white earbuds have been for the Apple iPod. Personal products, especially clothing and items you wear with clothing like watches, are good targets for visual hammers.

The iPod has 74 percent of the MP3-player market with nobody in second place unless you count SanDisk with its 7-percent share.

Traditionally, electric wires have been black. And since wires are a necessary evil, the idea was to make them disappear. And nothing disappears better than black.

Apple did the opposite, always a good strategy for developing a visual hammer. On the other hand, why call attention to the wires, the least important part of an MP3 player?

The white earbuds might be unimportant in the overall operation of

the device, but they let your friends and relatives know that you own an iPod, not some "imitation" brand.

The white earbuds, the contour bottle, the Swoosh, the Tri-Star and many other visual hammers mine the same conceptual field. They visualize the authenticity of the brands.

One brand that has done well with a visual hammer over the years is Campbell's soup, the leading brand of canned soup ever since records have been kept.

Campbell's red-and-white cans are an American icon, celebrated by Andy Warhol's 1960 silk-screen prints. But as you can see, the pressure

for change was apparently too much to resist. The red half is getting pushed off the can and the white half is getting eaten up by photos.

How long will it take for the Campbell Soup Company to turn its red-and-white icon into just another can of condensed soup?

At least Campbell Soup has managed to resist what many companies have not. That is, using color to differentiate its varieties, rather than to differentiate its brand.

I wonder how many consultants have advised Campbell to put its pea soup into green-and-white cans, its chicken-noodle soup into yellow-and-white cans and its French onion soup into brown-and-white cans?

Any trip down a supermarket aisle will demonstrate that color is used primarily to help consumers pick the right flavor from a single product line. A desirable goal, but secondary to the primary goal of identifying the brand in the first place.

And look at the effectiveness of Apple's stark white trademark. Originally, Apple used a trademark in six colors. When you compare the two marks, you might think the old six-color mark is much more attractive and it is. But "identity" is more important than attractiveness.

Apple's "white" visual is unusually effective in identifying Apple products even at a distance.

Apple also went the extra step in having the mark illuminated on its laptops. Also brilliant is the added touch of having a bite of the apple missing.

Compare BlackBerry with Apple. BlackBerry is a great name. It's unusual, it's alliterative and, in truth, BlackBerry is an even better name for a high-tech company than Apple.

One problem, however. How do you visualize the name?

BlackBerry's attempt to use blackberry seeds as an identifying device for its brand is pretty lame. The odd shapes used by BlackBerry don't look like much of anything.

Applebee's Neighborhood Grill & Bar is the largest casual-dining chain in America with 1,861 units and 2013 sales of $4.5 billion.

The Applebee's name was apparently created by combining a number of different words in order to find a euphonious pair.

In the alphabet, "a" is first and "b" is second so Applebee's sounds like a natural combination whereas Beeapple's sounds weird.

In addition, Applebee's wisely uses a red apple as a visual symbol for the brand. But why does Applebee's use a symbol that visualizes only half of the chain's brand name?

Applebee's could have used two symbols, a bee and an apple. That sounds logical, but visually it's wrong. One symbol is memorable; two symbols are confusing.

Another fruit brand name is "Pinkberry," a growing chain of upscale frozen desserts. There are 250 Pinkberry units selling desserts to a groupie-like following.

Blueberries are blue. Blackberries are black. But Pinkberry uses a logo that is primarily green?

That's not a good idea

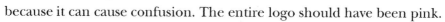

because it can cause confusion. The entire logo should have been pink.

One of Pinkberry's competitors, Red Mango, was actually first in the market, but has grown at a slower pace with only some 200 units to date.

But Red Mango's signage uses a fluorescent-red circle which is not only visually distinctive, but also reinforces the brand name.

Using a color as part of your brand name is often a good idea,

especially in a category that lacks "color" names. But keep in mind that consumers take brand names quite literally.

Your "color" brand needs a visual hammer that uses the same color as your brand name.

5

PRODUCT

THE IDEAL HAMMER.

If you can design your product so that it embodies a visual hammer, you can have a huge advantage in the marketplace.

Being first, of course, is particularly helpful. When you are first, a distinctive design is living proof of your leadership in the category.

No brand has exploited this advantage as well Rolex.

Its unique watchband is a status symbol as well as a visual hammer that positions Rolex as the leader in luxury watches.

As is true with many brands, Rolex was not the first luxury watch on the market. But it was the first luxury watch brand in the mind.

The arrival of a new category is usually marked by an avalanche of new brands. There have been thousands of brands of energy drinks and hundreds of brands of personal computers.

Take the latest high-technology product, the tablet computer. In January of 2011, more than 80 were introduced.

With so many brands in every category, the leading brand is unlikely to be the "best" product.

A good product, but not necessarily better than many other brands in the same category. "Life is unfair," said John F. Kennedy. That's true in marketing as well as in politics.

In spite of much evidence to the contrary, many marketing people assume the leading brand is the better product.

In the consumer field, for example, Consumer Reports, one of the few independent organizations that exhaustively tests products, often finds that secondary brands are clearly superior to market leaders.

In its coffee tests, McDonald's surprisingly beat Starbucks on taste.

What makes a brand a winner is the perception that it is the leader. It's a battle of perception rather than a battle of product quality.

As the market leader in high-end coffee, Starbucks is perceived by consumers to be better than other coffee brands.

In an emerging category with many brands fighting for a share of the consumer's mind, the brand that gets in the mind first and establishes a leadership position is almost impossible to dislodge. (Whether or not the brand was actually first is irrelevant.)

Kleenex in tissue. Heinz in ketchup. Hellmann's in mayonnaise.

Take words versus visuals. Words are weak. They're not memorable and they lack credibility. Conversely, visual hammers are memorable and emotional.

It's odd. Exaggeration works in visuals, but seldom works in verbals. The words, "Ralph Lauren is the brand that polo players wear," would generate nothing but yawns among consumers.

On the other hand, the polo-player visual which communicates exactly the same thing is a powerful device. It says that Ralph Lauren is the upscale brand, the leader in the category.

After all, next to yacht racing, polo is probably the world's most expensive sport, played mostly by millionaires and royalty.

What does the green alligator say about the Lacoste brand? Nothing, except the brand is Lacoste.

In essence, the alligator is a rebus, a picture that stands for a word. The polo player is a visual hammer that identifies Ralph Lauren as the leader.

Visuals are powerful because people tend to believe what they see and are skeptical of what they hear. Typical remark: "I know it's true, I saw it with my own eyes."

A visual hammer creates visibility for a brand far beyond what can be achieved by words alone.

Consider Rolls-Royce automobiles. Rolls-Royce does no advertising in the American market and it gets little publicity.

Yet the brand is well-known and is considered the best automobile brand in the world.

And it's not because America is being overrun by Rolls-Royces.

In 2014, only 900 were sold in America. Yet the grille of a Rolls is an unrivaled visual hammer.

Even though the average consumer sees very few Rolls-Royces each year, the few he or she does see make a lasting impression.

When you notice that unique grille, you don't say, what car is that? You say, that's a Rolls.

(That same year, 2014, there were 305,801 Mazda vehicles sold in America. How many Mazdas do you remember seeing on the road? No visual hammer and your brand becomes almost invisible.)

Porsche, Ferrari and Mini Cooper have taken the same approach. Design a visual difference into your automobiles and then maintain that difference over decades, not years.

Take the hybrid vehicle. There are some 18 hybrid brands on the American market, but one brand, Prius, has a dominant share.

In a recent year, Toyota Prius had 46 percent of the hybrid market.

Compare Honda with Toyota. Since 2002, the company has been selling the Honda Civic Hybrid in competition with the Toyota Prius.

And recently, Honda also began selling the Honda Accord hybrid.

Currently, consumers are buying eight times more Prius hybrids than Accord and Civic hybrids combined.

What's the difference? The Prius is a visual hammer. It looks like a hybrid, meaning that it looks totally different than other automobiles on the road. Smaller and quirkier, too. The Honda Civic hybrid looks like a Honda Civic. (The same is true for the Honda Accord hybrid which looks like a Honda Accord.)

Honda Civic hybrid.

In my neighborhood, there is a Honda Civic hybrid with the vanity license plate "HYBRID." People don't want a hybrid, they just want a car that looks like a hybrid.

The other half of the equation is the name "Prius," the verbal nail that gets hammered in the mind by the unique Prius visual.

(The Honda Civic hybrid has no visual hammer and no verbal nail.)

Look at the move into electric cars by almost every major automotive company. Among the first to hit the highways are the Chevrolet Volt and the Nissan Leaf.

Have you seen the new Nissan Leaf? They will be hard to see because they look the same as every other small car. It's too late to redesign the car, but what Nissan could have done is to produce Leafs for the first year in a single color.

My choice would have been "electric green." A simple step like this would have cost Nissan nothing.

Yet having all Nissan Leafs on the road in the color "green" would have greatly increased "street visibility" for the Leaf brand. With a name like "Leaf," what better color could you use?

You might think "early adopters" of the vehicle would complain about the lack of choice. But I doubt it.

Why did they buy a Leaf in the first place? It's not to save money; it's to make a statement. "Look at my car. I care about the environment." A distinctive color would make the statement even more dramatic.

You can also have negative visual hammers. Take the Smart car which was introduced in the American market in 2008.

Initially, the vehicle received a blast of favorable PR. Easy to drive, easy to park, good gas mileage. The first year the Smart car was on the market, 24,622 vehicles were sold.

Then Smart sales plummeted. To 14,595 vehicles the second year. And 5,927 vehicles the third year. (They have since inched their way up to 10,453 vehicles.)

It's easy to figure out what happened to Smart. Its street visibility was bound to create a lot of negative comments and criticism.

"Why pay full price for half a car?" Or "What did your Smart car look like before it was rear-ended by an 18-wheeler?"

Your product can sometimes look too different. It's not just what prospects think of your product; it's also what everybody else thinks of your product that matters, too.

Social pressure, amplified by social media, plays an important role in what brands consumers buy or don't buy.

People make statements with the brands they choose. They often want everybody to know what those brands are.

But in some categories, it's difficult to create a visual difference. You could make a man's dress shirt look different, but what man would want to wear a different-looking dress shirt?

Instead, Ralph Lauren put polo players on his shirts, the first dress shirts to carry a commercial message. Then he made a bold move by eliminating pockets, saving money and adding a touch of difference.

Sometimes you can make a product look different by doing the same thing, subtracting something.

Years ago, the creator of a candy-mint product made a deal with a manufacturer to press the mints into shape. But the manufacturer found the pressing process worked better with a hole in the middle.

Hence the brand name Life Savers and the verbal slogan "The candy mint with the hole."

A short time later, Life Savers was the No.1 mint-candy brand in America, a leadership position it has held ever since.

With such a mighty hammer, you might think it would be easy to take the Life Savers brand into other food and candy categories like gum and fruit punch.

As a Life Savers executive said at the time: "Our consumer dialogue indicates that the Life Savers brand name conveys more than merely 'candy with the hole.' It also means excellence in flavor, outstanding value and dependable quality."

Not so. Life Savers chewing gum, Life Savers fruit punch and other Life Savers line extensions are long gone, leaving Life Savers as the only "candy mint with the hole."

Even "Life Savers Holes" was a total disaster.

A visual hammer is not a sledge hammer. A visual hammer is more like an upholstery hammer

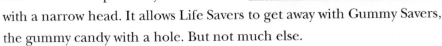

is more like an upholstery hammer with a narrow head. It allows Life Savers to get away with Gummy Savers, the gummy candy with a hole. But not much else.

What Life Savers did in candy, Cheerios has done in breakfast cereal. Most cereals are flakes of wheat, corn or oats. Distinguishable from one another on the outside of the box, but not in the bowl.

Not Cheerios, practically the only brand you can recognize in a bowl from twenty feet away.

"The cereal with the hole" is the brand's visual hammer which differentiates Cheerios from other cereals, most of them visually similar to each other.

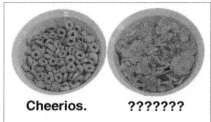

Cheerios.   ???????

So it should come as no surprise that Cheerios is the No.1 cereal brand, selling one out of every eight cereal boxes sold in supermarkets, twice the market share of the No.2 brand, Kellogg's Special K.

Another brand using a "holes" strategy is Thomas' English muffins. "The Original Nooks & Crannies English Muffins" is the verbal nail that exploits both the authenticity of the brand and its differentiation.

The stagecoach also hammers that verbal nail.

Then there was a shoe with the brand name "Beach," a shoe that had holes for ventilation and drainage.

Thank goodness they abandoned the Beach name and renamed the shoes "Crocs," a brand which caught on quickly and developed a loyal and vociferous following.

"People would say Man, those are ugly," said Crocs founder Duke Hanson, "and we would say, you

Ugly can be beautiful.

just got to try them on." Eventually that became the verbal nail for the Crocs brand: "Ugly can be beautiful."

The rise of Crocs was spectacular. From almost nothing in 2002 to $847.4 million in sales (and $168.2 million in net profits) in 2007, just five years later.

The fall of Crocs was just as spectacular as its rise. In 2008 and 2009, Crocs lost $229.2 million on sales of $1.4 billion.

It was a case of "too much, too soon." Not only did Crocs flood the market with a rainbow of colors, it quickly added many other styles: flip-flops, sandals and even ladies heels.

Especially troublesome was the fact that many of the expanded styles were attractive and fashionable, which undercut the brand's verbal nail, "Ugly can be beautiful."

In addition, Crocs spent many millions of dollars buying up other companies like EXO Italia which made vinyl shoes and Fury Hockey which made sticks, gloves, pants

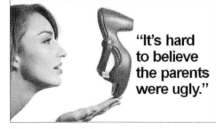

"It's hard to believe the parents were ugly."

and elbow pads. There was even talk of launching Crocs clothing. (Holes in clothing? That doesn't make any sense.)

Fortunately, Crocs liquidated most of these line extensions and in 2010 Crocs became profitable again and has remained profitable.

Even the tiniest of holes can serve as the source for a visual hammer. A brand with a fantastic track record is Geox, the shoe that breathes.

Currently the company sells more than $1 billion worth every year. Even more spectacular is its profit margins. Over the past five years, they have been averaging about 14 percent a year.

Geox shoes are a very good example of the power of a verbal/visual approach to building a brand. If you just focused on the benefits of the Geox brand, you might come up with a slogan like "The healthiest, most-comfortable shoe you can buy."

That says it all, right?

It sure does, but it rules out the possibility of a visual hammer.

How do you visualize "healthiest" and "comfortable?"

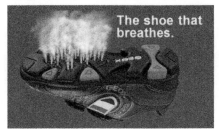

The shoe that breathes.

You can't. But "the shoe that breathes" lends itself to a spectacular visual for the Geox brand.

Without the visual hammer, the verbal claim would fall totally flat. "A shoe that breathes? That's ridiculous. Shoes don't breathe."

Visual hammers are particularly effective for high-end fashion brands. They tell friends how smart (or how dumb) you are.

Take ultra-expensive Louis Vuitton handbags. They have a unique multiple-logotype design that anyone can recognize.

In certain circles, owning a Louis Vuitton handbag is one of those possessions a woman has to have.

In Tokyo, according to one report, more than 90 percent of women in their twenties own a Louis Vuitton handbag.

If the handbag itself weren't quite so "outlandish," Louis Vuitton sales wouldn't be nearly as high.

Products should be attractive, but it's more important that they be distinctive, as the success of Louis Vuitton and Crocs demonstrates.

In Interbrand's latest report, Louis Vuitton is the world's 17th most valuable brand, worth $24.9 billion. The 38th most valuable brand in the world is Gucci, another example of a brand with a visual hammer.

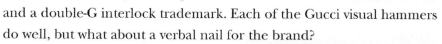

As a matter of fact, two visual hammers. Red-and-green stripes and a double-G interlock trademark. Each of the Gucci visual hammers do well, but what about a verbal nail for the brand?

Both Gucci and Louis Vuitton would greatly benefit from verbal expressions of their positions.

Study the fashion ads in a copy of Vogue. Like this Gucci advertisement, you'll find most of

them are totally visual, with the copy limited to the name of the brand.

There are excellent opportunities to "break the fashion pattern" by developing verbal nails that could be visualized.

That's what Barack Obama did in 2008. His Presidential election campaign captured the attention of the marketing community.

At the Association of National Advertisers conference that year, Barack Obama was voted as the "Marketer of the Year."

His 2008 political campaign combined a memorable nail, "Change we can believe in," with a memorable hammer, the flagship rising sun.

The combination produced an election victory few pundits would have predicted just a year earlier.

For a virtually-unknown first-time senator, a member of a minority group and a man with an unusual name to be elected President of the United States is a testament to the effectiveness of the hammer-and-nail marketing approach.

But the question arose, what should Barack Obama's 2012 campaign focus on? Not "Change."

Why is this so? Because "Change" would have implied that he had not done a very good job in his first four years.

What Obama needed to imply was that everything was going well, but that the job was only half done.

Or as he said in a State of the Union speech, "We've come too far to turn back now." Then the 2012 campaign used the word "Forward."

In other words, go forward with Barack Obama or go backward with Mitt Romney and the Republicans.

That made it two in a row for the 2008 "Marketer of the Year."

6

PACKAGE

MAKE IT DIFFERENT.

Most brands are focused on product. The emphasis is on developing and producing a product demonstrably superior to competition.

The product's packaging is often overlooked as a branding element. Sure, the package itself is loaded with copy explaining the virtues of the brand. But the actual package, its shape and its composition, can be an important visual element.

Too often, package design is delegated to manufacturing experts who crave efficiency, cost and utility.

Hellmann's is a good example. It's the leading mayonnaise brand but its packaging is mediocre.

Hellmann's looks like all the other jars of mayonnaise.

On the other hand, Heinz "octagon" ketchup bottles are an example of how innovative packaging can help build a dominant brand.

Its unique glass bottle with its octagon shape is instantly recognized by most consumers. It's almost as well-known as Coke's contour bottle.

Even high-end white-table-cloth restaurants will put Heinz bottles on their tables, one of the few food brands that get treated this way.

For years, Heinz was marketed as "The slowest ketchup in the West," one of the most effective verbal nails ever developed for a food brand.

According to the company, the ketchup exits its iconic glass bottle at .028 miles per hour.

If the viscosity is greater than this speed, it is rejected for sale to consumers.

Currently, Heinz is marketing larger-size plastic ketchup bottles which presumably can be sold for lower prices. But like Coca-Cola and its contour bottle, the Heinz octagon bottle remains an important visual hammer for the brand, even though relatively few are sold.

How would you design a pair of pantyhose to look different? (Most women want them to look invisible.)

If you can't make your product look different, you can still make its packaging look different.

Years ago, Hanes Corporation marketed Hanes, the leading brand of pantyhose. But the Hanes brand was sold in department stores and the corporation wanted a second brand for supermarkets.

The name Hanes picked was brilliant and the brand's packaging (the visual hammer) was even better.

The double-entendre "L'eggs" was a perfect name for pantyhose sold in supermarkets. And the plastic-egg package was a killer hammer for the brand. L'eggs was so successful it became the country's largest-selling pantyhose brand.

But apparently the plastic-egg packaging was expensive, so at some point in time, L'eggs was moved from plastic to cardboard.

That's not always a bad idea.

Launch.   **Current.**

In some categories, it might make sense to launch a new brand in ultra-expensive packaging. Then, after the brand becomes successful, start using conventional packaging to keep the brand's price reasonable.

Another category that gets a host of new brands almost every year is beverages. One recently-successful beverage brand is Vitaminwater.

So successful that in 2007 the Coca-Cola Company bought Glaceau, the maker of Vitaminwater and Smartwater, for $4.1 billion in cash, by far the Coca-Cola company's largest acquisition to date.

The Vitaminwater bottles are perhaps the most visually-arresting beverage packages ever conceived.

They remind consumers of prescription drugs on a pharmacy's shelf, just the right visual concept for a "vitamin" beverage.

Whether or not the Vitaminwater brand is worth $4.1 billion is another matter, but you have to admire the brand's visual look.

But beware. While the Vitaminwater bottle was designed to look symbolically like a bottle of vitamins, that's exactly the wrong strategy to use if you're not first.

If you're not first in a new category, you want to design your bottle so it looks like the bottle doesn't belong in the category at all.

Take vodka, one of the oldest beverages. Some Polish vodka brands go back centuries, notable Zubrowka and Starka from the 16th century and Goldwasser from the early 17th century.

Compared to these and a number of Russian brands, Absolut from Sweden is an infant, not introduced until the spring of 1979.

In spite of its late start, the Absolut bottle would become one of the most famous visual hammers in the world.

Instead of designing Absolut to look like a vodka bottle, designers made it look like an apothecary jar you'd find in a pharmacy.

Swedish advertising executive Gunnar Broman brought the bottle and the proposed name to the advertising agency N.W. Ayer for its help in launching the new vodka.

"It looks like one of those medical bottles," was their first response. "Like for blood plasma or something." Another chimed in, 'You can't sell a thing like that. Well, you might be able to sell Absolut to doctors."

Eventually, the account ended up at TBWA which made the Absolut bottle the star of a long-running advertising campaign which has won many awards. Typical advertising headlines: "Absolut attraction." And: "Absolut perfection." Also: "Absolut treasure."

How effective was the bottle advertising? Absolut vodka became the No.1 imported vodka in America and one of the ten best-selling distilled-spirit brands in the world.

Advertising Age selected the Absolut "bottle" campaign as one of the top 100 advertising campaigns of the 20th century. (No.7.)

If the bottle was the visual hammer, what was Absolut's verbal nail? It was Absolut's high price.

Compared to Smirnoff, the leading vodka and the largest-selling spirit brand in America, Absolut was 65-percent more expensive.

That's a big price difference for a product which by law must be "colorless, tasteless and odorless."

But why didn't Absolut mention its higher price in its advertising? In truth, there's no easy way to say "more expensive" in your advertising without sounding gauche.

Furthermore, vodka drinkers will get the high-price message as soon as they purchase a bottle of Absolut in a liquor store or order an Absolut martini in a high-end restaurant.

Another unusual fact. Why are so many visual hammers developed by startups and so few visual hammers developed by large companies?

Where are visual hammers for big brands like IBM, Xerox, Verizon, Hewlett-Packard, General Electric, Intel, Cisco, Oracle?

When a big company owns a visual hammer, it's usually because it was a legacy hammer created several generations back. The Mercedes Tri-Star. The Rolex watchband. Campbell's soup can.

Big companies don't usually make big marketing decisions without first conducting extensive research. And consumers don't generally like anything that's too different.

"We spent $65,000 on research and it was quite negative," said Michel Roux, president of the American company that was planning to import Absolut.

"It said the bottle would be lost on the shelf, the name was nothing like vodka and Sweden was not seen as a vodka-producing country."

As a psychological principle, consumers like "better," but they don't like "different." Marketing principles are the opposite. As a marketing principle, "better" doesn't work, but "different" does.

If you can't make the bottle different, maybe you can make the glass the product is served in different.

That's the strategy employed by Stella Artois when it arrived in the American market back in 1999.

To introduce the new beer, Interbrew, the Belgian brewer of Stella Artois, limited distribution to 20 exclusive bars and clubs in Manhattan.

Furthermore, Stella Artois charged almost 20 percent more for a keg than its Holland competitor did for a keg of Heineken.

That took courage since Stella is the Bud of Belgium, so ordinary that fast-food restaurants sell it in plastic cups to high-school students.

No plastic cups for Stella Artois beer in the American market. Interbrew provided the bars with unique, gold-tipped chalice glasses and a lesson in Stella Artois etiquette. Beer was to be served between 36 and 38 degrees F. and the foam must be shaved off with a spoon.

(Actually the Stella Artois glasses were no special deal. In Belgium, every beer has its own unique glass designed to highlight the brand's special flavor and Stella Artois was no exception.)

With its chalice hammer, Stella Artois sales took off. The brand was expanded into national distribution and eventually into supermarkets and other retail outlets.

Today, Stella Artois is the fifth largest-selling imported-beer. Stella cans on supermarket shelves even feature its chalice glass.

What's missing from the Stella story is a powerful verbal nail.

"Perfection has its price," its current position, adequately describes the Stella brand, but sacrifices memorability and uniqueness.

That's a potential problem for Stella Artois and many other brands with strong visual hammers and weak verbal nails.

Because the strength of a visual hammer is partially based on its shock value, a visual hammer over time will slowly lose some of its marketing effectiveness as the shock value tapers off.

The reverse is true for a verbal nail. Unless you are using one of the seven words you can't use on network television, it's hard to find a combination of words with the shock value of an arresting visual.

One exception might be French Connection. In 2001, the company began branding its clothes in the United Kingdom as "fcuk."

Apparently the fcuk acronym was discovered when a message was sent from its Hong Kong outlet to its United Kingdom outlet entitled "FCHK to FCUK."

Though the company insists that FCUK is an acronym for French Connection United Kingdom, its similarity to another word caused considerable controversy.

French Connection exploited the media attention by producing a range of T-shirts with messages such as: "fcuk fashion," "fcuk football," "fcuk on the beach." And similar thoughts.

Unlike visual hammers, verbal nails actually become more credible as time passes. Initially, consumers are skeptical of claims like BMW's "ultimate driving machine."

But over time and with repeated repetitions, the credibility of a verbal claim actually increases.

The first time you heard "Just do it," you probably thought, Huh. What does Nike mean by that?

But eventually, "Just do it" because more than just a Nike slogan. It became a rallying cry for the younger generation. The more people who identify with a slogan, the more powerful that slogan becomes.

Marketers make a major mistake when they copy-test verbal slogans before using them. It doesn't matter what a consumer's first reaction is.

What matters is how consumers feel after they have heard your advertising slogan 50 or 100 times.

But how can you know in advance how they might feel? You can't. But one rule of thumb is to make sure your visual hammer is strongly linked to your verbal nail.

Marketing is like woodworking. No matter how good your hammer, you have to consistently hit your nail to make your brand successful.

The Stella glass is a great hammer, but it has little connection with the Stella nail, "Perfection has its price."

Sure, if you think about it, you get the connection. Expensive glass equals expensive beer which is the price you pay for perfection.

But to work, the connection has to be instantaneous, with no time left for thinking. Stella Artois needs to use the word "glass" or something similar in its verbal nail.

Notice the difference between the Stella Artois glass and the Evian "mountains." The mountains are more than a nice visual to decorate the label. The mountains are the  hammer and "Natural spring water from the French Alps" is the nail.

It's the combination, the mountain hammer and the French Alps nail, that has made Evian the best-selling expensive water.

One of the most unusual packaging hammers is the swing-top cap on Grolsch premium pilsner which looks both expensive and obsolete.

Yet it's one reason why Grolsch is the 21st largest producer of beer in the world and second only to Heineken in Holland, its home country.

Like the Jack Daniel's bottle, the Grolsch swing-top cap connotes authenticity and old-fashioned quality. Too bad Grolsch doesn't nail a verbal idea along with its swing-top hammer. Still, Grolsch Brewery was bought in 2007 by SABMiller for $1.2 billion.

Not bad for an old-fashioned beer brand with a swing-top cap.

An old-fashioned packaging concept that has created a stir in the distilled-spirits business is the dripping red-wax seal on Maker's Mark bourbon. Not only is the red-wax seal distinctive, it's also a legal trademark for the brand.

The dripping red wax is the hammer, but what's the nail?

The name, Maker's Mark, which communicates the idea of bourbon hand-crafted by artisans.

Marker's Mark has experienced more than 30 years of double-digit growth and claims a 70-percent market share in fine bourbon.

Another packaging visual hammer is wrapping the brand in paper bound by gold tape. Lea & Perrins did that with Worcestershire sauce, a brand with a reported 97-percent market share.

What's the nail? The word "original" on the Lea & Perrins package which together with the brand's dominant market share reinforces its position as the leader in Worcestershire sauce.

When a brand has such a huge market share, it is almost immune to competition. (What's true in Worcestershire sauce is also true in personal-computer operating systems. For decades, Windows has had a 90-percent market share.)

Pom Wonderful, a brand of pomegranate juice, is another example of a brand with a packaging visual hammer. With a shape like no other, the Pom Wonderful bottle is truly unique and different.

One particularly effective billboard for the Pom Wonderful brand has the Pom bottle dressed in a superhero's cape.

The brand's verbal nail: "The antioxidant superpower."

That sounds like a slogan that could last a lifetime.

7

ACTION

MORE EFFECTIVE THAN STILLS.

Visual hammers involving action, movement or demonstration are considerably more effective than static hammers, or still pictures. The advertising medium that can best handle "action" is television.

That's one reason why the TV medium has continued to prosper while print and radio have declined.

In the year 2014, more advertising money was spent on television than on newspapers, magazines and radio combined.

Dove soap is one-fourth moisturizing lotion. Years ago, a typical print ad tried to exploit this feature with a photograph of a woman in a bathtub and the slogan "Dove creams your skin while you wash."

But it was TV that built Dove into the market leader, with a 24-percent share of the bar-soap market.

What visual hammered the Dove brand into the mind?

A hand pouring the moisturizing lotion into a bar of Dove soap. Utterly simple, incredibly effective.

What's the difference between the words, "one-fourth moisturizing lotion," and demonstrating the words?

Nothing. Both the verbal words and the visual images communicate exactly the same idea. The difference is shock value and memorability.

The average person reads or hears about 42,000 words every day. How many of those words do most people remember? Very few.

Furthermore, they don't necessarily believe many of the words they do hear on radio or read in print.

A television visual demonstration, especially one that contains an element of shock, is not only memorable, it's also believable.

A visual "shock" doesn't have to be something as dramatic as parting the Red Sea.

Television is an intimate medium. Johnny Carson used to get a big laugh by raising his eyebrows. Today, Jon Stewart or Stephen Colbert often do the same.

As television moves to high definition and sets get more authentic, the potential for subtlety increases.

A visual "shock" can also be achieved by juxtapositioning elements. Pouring a cup of moisturizing lotion into a bar of Dove soap creates visual tension or shock.

Is a Mini Cooper a shocking vehicle? Not really, it's just another small car. Is a Ford Excursion a shocking vehicle? Not really, it's just another big sport-utility vehicle.

In the year 2002, when BMW introduced the Mini Cooper in the American market, it put a number of Minis on top of Ford Excursions and drove them around city roads and streets with a message: "What are you doing for fun this weekend?"

The cars mounted on top of Ford Excursions dramatized how "mini" a Mini Cooper really is.

Another example of juxtapositioning is Tropicana's "straw in the orange." Neither a straw nor an orange is visually shocking, but the combination certainly is.

It's especially so on TV where the viewer can see a person sticking a straw into an orange and then drinking from the straw. You can't get juice out of an orange by sucking on a straw, you might be thinking. True, but a visual can have emotional power whether it's true or not.

The viewer thinks, Tropicana contains the juice of whole oranges because it's "not from concentrate."

Just as shocking is the brand's market share. Although Tropicana is premium priced, its market share is about 30 percent.

Recently, Tropicana decided to drop its "straw in the orange" visual hammer on its packaging and focus on a verbal approach.

Along with its new approach came a new package design without the straw. The new campaign was based on the word "squeeze."

As explained by the president of Tropicana North America, as reported in The New York Times, "The whole idea of squeeze is to play up the functional benefit of orange juice in providing fruit for people's daily diets and the emotional connection people have with Tropicana."

"Squeeze" said the chairman of Tropicana's advertising agency, "is the process by which we get our product and the hug."

He continued, "There was this notion of owning a simple word that would communicate the love, the care, in the Obama moment we're all going through," added the chairman.

This is left-brain verbal thinking, focused on the rational power of words to incite emotion instead of the inherently-emotional power of visuals like the straw-in-the-orange.

What visual could Tropicana have used to illustrate "squeeze?" A consumer hugging an orange? I think not.

As you probably know, consumer reaction to the new Tropicana campaign was swift and vicious.

I've never seen such an outpouring of negative comments. In two months, sales dropped 20 percent.

The negative reaction was so swift and dramatic that Tropicana dropped the new packaging and brought back "straw in the orange."

Actually, Tropicana came back with two visual hammers. The straw in the orange and a zipper that symbolically opens on the carton to allow 16 fresh-picked oranges to jump inside the Tropicana package.

Both are nice visuals, but are two hammers better than one? No. They just create visual confusion for the Tropicana brand.

Another emotionally-potent visual hammer is the yellow pages logo with the verbal nail "let your fingers do the walking."

Again, the walking fingers were particularly effective on television, although most of the usage of the yellow-pages symbol was in print.

Today, Google has just about killed the market for yellow-page advertising as more and more consumers use their fingers to do their searching online. Google built its brand with a clean white page and a search box. Nothing fancy and always the same.

But a few days of the year, Google changes its logotype to celebrate special occasions, like one used for the Fourth of July.

The images used to be static, but recently Google has been using subtle "action" to dramatize those special occasions.

This "action" idea would probably never occur to most business executives who are highly verbal.

They think in words, not pictures. They assume the two are interchangeable. To communicate the essence of a visual, one just needs to verbalize it. Not true.

A visual activates the right side of your brain, the emotional side. A verbal activates the left side of your brain, the rational side.

Aleve has developed a great hammer (2 Aleve versus 8 Tylenol Extra for all day relief) and a great nail (If you could take fewer pills, why wouldn't you?) But they are using the nail primarily in print.

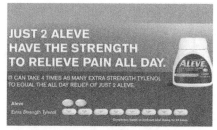

On television, Aleve uses "slice of life" commercials where users talk about the benefits of the pain reliever instead of demonstrating them with a powerful visual hammer.

Seeing two Aleve pills compared to eight Tylenol pills effectively demonstrates the difference. The more specific you can be the better.

Perhaps no series of television commercials have demonstrated the power of a visual hammer like the Marlboro commercials in the 1960s. All cowboys, all horses, all action, few words.

The Marlboro music, the theme from the motion picture The Magnificent Seven starring Yul Brynner and Steve McQueen, also contributed to the emotional effectiveness of the commercials.

Music doesn't lie dormant, frozen in time, like the words on a page. Music is aural action. It's always moving, going someplace. At times in a hurry, at times at a languid pace. But always in motion.

It's the difference between a sheet of music and music itself.

The 1971 ban on televised tobacco advertising put an end to the Marlboro commercials.

But they are still worth studying today to understand the emotional effectiveness of a television hammer augmented with a musical theme.

8

FOUNDER

NATURAL-BORN HAMMERS.

We live in a celebrity-obsessed world. The media is fascinated with the lives of the rich and famous. Even ordinary people can become celebrities as long as they are infamous.

The most successful magazine in America is not a news magazine, a sports magazine or a financial magazine.

It's a celebrity magazine, People, which carries more advertising pages than any other magazine.

Don't blame the media. It's consumers who buy the fan magazines and flock to the television shows like Celebrity Apprentice or Keeping up the Kardashians that should get the credit, or the blame, for our obsession with celebrities.

Even business tycoons are getting their share of publicity.

It's surprising how many corporate CEOs are getting to be as famous as their companies.

Michael Dell of Dell, Howard Schultz of Starbucks, Richard Branson of Virgin, Larry Ellison of Oracle, Mark Zuckerberg of Facebook.

If you want to make your company famous, we often advise clients, then you also have to make your chief executive famous too.

The founder of a company benefits from celebrity worship in two ways: (1) Everyone wants to know something about the person who runs a company.

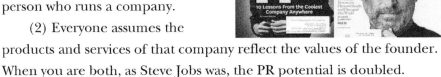

(2) Everyone assumes the products and services of that company reflect the values of the founder. When you are both, as Steve Jobs was, the PR potential is doubled.

Celebrity worship is a relatively new development; founder worship is not. Henry Ford founded the Ford Motor Company more than a century ago and the company still uses his signature as its trademark.

Why would Ford, a modern corporation with the marketing goal of trying to establish a reputation for the latest in automotive technology, still use as its logotype the old-fashioned signature of its founder, Henry Ford?

Doesn't it make the company look out of date?

Perhaps. But the old-fashioned signature also provides legitimacy. Any company that has been around as long as the Ford Motor Company must be doing something right.

Legitimacy is especially important in industries that sell "invisible" products. What do you get when you buy a life insurance policy?

You might spend thousands of dollars and have nothing to show for your money except a pile of paper.

The legitimacy and financial stability of the insurance company is an important aspect of your purchase.

That's why in 1862 the founders of a Boston insurance company borrowed the name of one of the 56 signers of the 1776 Declaration of Independence.

Today, John Hancock Financial Services is a major American insurance company, although currently owned by a Canadian company.

Of the 56 original signers of the Declaration of Independence, John Hancock is the most famous.

Hancock's large, flamboyant signature (nearly five inches wide) dwarfs the other 55 signers.

Imagine? A visual hammer on the Declaration of Independence.

Jack Daniel's is the best-selling whiskey in the world and the fourth best-selling liquor brand in America (after Smirnoff, Bacardi and Captain Morgan rum.) One reason for its success is its age.

The distillery was founded in the year 1866, just after the Civil War. The first distillery licensed in the country.

Every category is different, but in the beverage category, old is good. Not bad. Witness the success of brands like Old Grand-Dad, Old Crow, Old Forester and Olde English.

And witness the failure of New Coke. Once a beverage brand has become established, change is only going to cause confusion.

In beverages of all types, it's not enough to be old. You also need to communicate the concept that your brand has never changed.

Jack Daniel's has done that in various ways including this one.

But it's the black label itself that's the visual hammer.

The label looks old and the old-fashioned look is reinforced with the words: "Old Time. Old No. 7 brand." On the back of the label is the message: "Whiskey made as our fathers made it for 7 generations."

Jack Daniel's has also managed to portray the town of Lynchburg, Tennessee, where the distillery is located, as old and never changing.

As one advertisement said: "Jack Daniel's. Enjoyed in 135 countries, made in a town with one stoplight."

Jack Daniel, the founder, and the black label are the visual hammers and the "first American whiskey" is the verbal nail although that verbal idea is not stated explicitly.

Obviously there are a lot of less-successful liquor brands trying to create an old-fashioned look and reputation.

But it's not enough to have old-fashioned labels and old-fashioned names like Ancient Age and Old Fitzgerald bourbon. You also need an old-fashioned visual hammer.

Compare Yuengling beer to Jack Daniel's whiskey. D.G. Yuengling of Pottsville, Pennsylvania, was founded in 1829, more than three decades before Mr. Daniel started his distillery.

While Jack Daniel's is the largest-selling whiskey, Yuengling is back in 19th place in beer. The name "Yuengling," an Anglicized version of the German term for "young man," is a weak brand name.

And unfortunately, the name doesn't sound German. Nor in English does it connote much of anything or sound nice.

The verbal nail "America's oldest brewery" has potential, but the brand would need a strong visual hammer to realize that potential.

In 2010, President Barack Obama sent a case of Yuengling to Canadian Prime Minister Stephen Harper to cover a friendly wager on the outcome of the Winter Olympic hockey final.

That's the kind of endorsement and PR the brand is going to need to pump up sales. But it's not going to be easy when you have a name like Yuengling and no visual hammer.

If Yuengling beer is a bad name, how about John Schnatter's pizza? Fortunately, Mr. Schnatter chose a different name.

He called his chain, "Papa John's" in order to compete with Pizza Hut and Domino's.

And he has done well. In the American market, Papa John's has higher annual per-unit sales than its two major competitors.

Here are 2013 per-unit sales of Papa John's compared with Domino's Pizza and Pizza Hut.

Papa John's went upscale with a verbal nail it has used consistently for decades. "Better ingredients. Better pizza. Papa John's."

Papa John's $788,000
Pizza Hut $771,000
Domino's $731,000

But the visual hammer in the television commercials is the real secret of Papa John's success.

With a name like Papa John, you would expect to see an older, Italian-looking man with grey hair and a handlebar mustache.

What you don't expect to see is John Schnatter, who looks like a clean-shaven college student with a rah-rah enthusiasm for his brand.

Papa John is the visual hammer. That's what creates the visual shock that hammers in the verbal nail: "Better ingredients. Better pizza."

A good picture, someone said, would be a row of West Point cadets lined up perfectly. A great picture would be that same line-up with a pigeon sitting on the shoulder of one of the cadets. The pigeon is the hammer that creates the visual shock.

Nobody looked as shocking as Harland Sanders, the founder of Kentucky Fried Chicken, now KFC.

Known as Colonel Sanders, he traveled the country in a white suit and black string tie promoting his secret recipe of 11 herbs and spices. "Finger lickin' good" was the

verbal nail and Colonel Sanders was the visual hammer, a combination that created the largest chicken chain in the country.

(Harland Sanders was a real Kentucky Colonel, the highest award given to individuals by the state. Other Kentucky Colonels include Elvis Presley, Bill Clinton, Betty White and Tiger Woods.)

For a number of years KFC has struggled with its marketing and its product offering. "Fried" chicken has developed a reputation as unhealthy, one reason for using the initials, KFC.

But unless a company or brand is exceptionally well-known (IBM, AT&T, GE and a few others), it is usually a mistake to change a brand's name to initials.

Sure, KFC is a well-known nickname for the brand, but in the mind the initials serve as short-hand for Kentucky Fried Chicken. It's hard to run away from what you stand for. And KFC stands for "fried chicken."

KFC has also been running from one ad campaign to another with little continuity or success.

What's wrong with all of these slogans? None suggest a visual.

And without a visual, almost any marketing campaign is doomed from the beginning.

2009:
Taste the unfried side of KFC.
2010:
So good.
2013:
I ate the bones.
2014:
How do you do KFC?

(Colonel Sanders' picture is on the building, but he no longer serves as the visual hammer for KFC's marketing.)

KFC's latest slogan, "How do you do KFC?," is a say-nothing slogan that also communicates nothing.

"So good" might be a minimally-effective marketing slogan except one thing. Too many other brands have used similar slogans.

Campbell's soup... "M'm..M'm good."

Maxwell House..... "Good to the last drop."

Delta .... "Good goes around."

GE .... "We bring good things to life."

Visual hammers and verbal nails need to be unique and different. "Good" is a worn-out word.

Except, of course, for those brands that have pre-empted the "good" concept including Campbell's soup and Kentucky Fried Chicken whose original slogan was "Finger-lickin' good."

So how do you fix a brand that has lost its way? One of the best ways is to back track. Go back in history to reclaim aspects of the brand that made it successful in the first place.

One visual aspect of the KFC brand that almost every consumer identifies with is Colonel Sanders in his white suit and white goatee.

The best brands are those where every aspect of the brand is "locked" together, which, of course, is what this book is all about.

But that concept also applies to the name of the brand.

Drive past a KFC restaurant and what do you see? A picture of Colonel Sanders.

So why wouldn't you call the
restaurant chain "Colonel Sanders" chicken? That locks the brand name to the visual hammer. And why wouldn't you bring back the original slogan, "Finger-lickin' good....with 11 herbs and spices?" I would.

One advantage of using a dead founder like Colonel Sanders as your visual hammer is the fact that he will never get into a scandal and damage your brand. That's not always the case with a live founder.

Martha Stewart spent five months in jail in an insider-trading case for "obstructing justice, conspiracy and making false statements."

Did the bad publicity hurt the Martha Stewart brand? In the short term, sure, but it didn't kill it.

The brand today is probably no worse off than it was before the trial started in the year 2004.

That's not to say the brand is healthy. In the last ten years,
Martha Stewart Living Omnimedia, had revenues of $2.3 billion and managed to lose $201 million.

Why is the company in trouble when Martha Stewart is one of the best-known women in America? That's the paradox of marketing.

It doesn't matter how "well known" you are. The thing that matters is "what" you are well known for.

Colonel Sanders is known for chicken. Papa John is known for pizza. Jack Daniel is known for whiskey. John Hancock is known for insurance. But what is Martha Steward known for?

The "Omni" in her firm's name, Martha Stewart Living Omnimedia, illustrates the weakness in her brand.

Martha Stewart is known for everything…and nothing. Magazines, books, television, radio, pots & pans, towels, sheets, paint, you name it.

When you put your name on everything as Martha Stewart has done, you usually wind up standing for nothing.

Another founder who is floundering is Hugh Hefner of Playboy.

His magazine made a big splash when Playboy was first published in December of 1953.

For years, Playboy magazine was the largest-circulation men's publication in the country.

But like Martha Stewart, Hugh Hefner couldn't resist expanding.

Over the years there has been Playboy clubs, Playboy cable channels, Playboy television shows, Playboy hotels, Playboy books, Playboy videos and hundreds of Playboy products licensed to companies including the makers of condoms and T-shirts.

What there hasn't been much of is Playboy profits.

In ten years from 2001 to 2010, Playboy Enterprises, had revenues of $3.0 billion and losses of $293 million.

Playboy went public in 1971 for $23.50 a share. It was taken private in 2011 by a group led by Hugh Hefner for $6.15 a share.

(After 40 years, that's not much of a return on your investment.)

In those four decades, Playboy and its founder Hugh Hefner have received reams of publicity leading people to believe that the company must be fabulously successful.

But publicity success is not always equivalent to financial success. Take Richard Branson, the founder of Virgin, a megabrand that has spawned hundreds of different companies worldwide.

Nobody, but nobody, has received as much favorable publicity as Richard Branson. But PR success is no magic wand that can create instant money. Many hundreds of Virgin companies are reportedly big losers in the marketplace.

Then too, most of his Virgin companies are private, so it's hard to tell whether they are successful.

I was able to track down only one major Virgin company that reported revenues and profits.

That was Virgin Australia Holdings, the airline company. In the past ten years, the company has had $26.8 billion in revenues and managed to lose $11.9 million.

Richard Branson is a mighty hammer, but like Martha Stewart and Hugh Hefner he is using his PR skills to hit too many nails at once.

What's a Virgin anyway? For one thing, it's an airline. Actually, it's three airlines, one in the United Kingdom, one in Australia and one in America. None of these three airlines seem to be making any net profits.

Compare Virgin's money-losing Australian airline with Southwest. In the past ten years, Southwest Airlines had revenues of $117.0 billion and profits of $4.1 billion or a profit margin of 3.5 percent.

Nor do other Virgin companies appear to be making much progress. When have you last seen someone order a Virgin cola, a Virgin vodka, a Virgin energy shot or unscrew a bottle of Virgin wine?

Yet Branson has an enormous impact on the marketing community. "If Virgin can do it, why can't we?"

That's the attitude of many marketing people worldwide. But few marketing people seem to have checked the actual results of Virgin's line extensions. If they did, they might realize it's not a model to emulate.

Then there's the question of what happens when Richard Branson is no longer around to do PR?

Many visual hammers don't survive into the second generation. Take Frank Perdue, the man behind the success of Perdue chicken.

In 1953, when Frank Perdue became president and chief executive of Perdue Farms, the chicken-breeding company was doing only about $5 million in chicken sales a year.

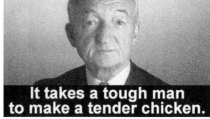

In 1970, Perdue Farms launched its first television campaign featuring its sharp-featured president.

Sales skyrocketed. By 1988, Perdue revenues reached $975 million. Today, they are $3.2 billion.

While the Perdue Farms company has survived and prospered, its tough-man hammer and its tender-chicken nail have not.

In 1994, Frank's son James took over as spokesperson for the brand, but he didn't have the tough-guy personality of his father.

Nor did his verbal, "A healthy obsession with chicken," have the memorability of "It takes a tough man to make a tender chicken."

Can a personal hammer survive into the second or even the third generation? It certainly can in politics.

Witness the political success of Hillary Clinton, Jeb Bush, Rand Paul, Al Gore, Andrew Cuomo and other sons, daughters, wives and husbands of famous political figures. Companies can do the same.

But in Perdue's case, perhaps there was too much emphasis on the hammer and not enough on the nail.

A "tender" chicken is a generic claim that could be used by almost any producer. What might have worked better was the visual difference that played a big part in the success of the Perdue brand.

Perdue chickens were fed marigold leaves to turn their skins yellow. Instead of "tender" chicken it might have been better to use "golden" chicken as a verbal nail.

Whenever you have a choice, it's always better to select the claim that is visually different even though it's not verbally better.

Visuals are more powerful than words.

No person can live forever, but a founder hammer can exist for several lifetimes. So how does a brand make the transition from a live founder to a dead historical figure?

One thing that is helpful is using a stylized cartoon drawing of the founder rather than a photograph. Cartoons don't usually work on TV, but on signs, on the Internet and in print, they work very well.

Another thing that is helpful is a difference in clothing (white suit & black string tie for Colonel Sanders) or a difference in facial hair (mustache & goatee for Jack Daniel.)

Take Orville Redenbacher, the visual hammer for the popping-corn brand which has survived the death of its founder. It didn't work when they tried to use him as a cartoon on television, but in print, on the Internet and on the package, Orville Redenbacher with his black glasses and bow tie is still alive and effective as a visual hammer.

The verbal nail for the brand is its high price. Initially, the words "Gourmet popping corn" were set in larger type than the brand name, followed by the claim, "World's most-expensive popping corn."

Today, the brand is focused on "gourmet." And it doesn't just say gourmet, the brand has a visual difference. Since it uses larger popping kernels, Orville Redenbacher's popping corn pops bigger and fluffier.

Despite the advantages a higher price can bring, many companies overlook the simple idea of charging more for their products.

That's the idea that built brands like Häagen-Dazs, Rolex, Evian, Starbucks, Grey Goose and many others.

But it's not enough to be expensive. Your brand also has to be the first brand in the category to be "perceived" as expensive.

In marketing terminology, Orville Redenbacher's popping corn "pre-empted" the expensive popping-corn category.

Brands that follow might be just as expensive, but they will never become "the" gourmet popping corn.

Another founder who has legs even though he departed the scene in 2008 is Paul Newman, creator of Newman's Own line of food & beverage products. Since 1982, Newman's Own has contributed over $400 million to charities.

What made Newman such an effective visual was his steely blue eyes and good-humored charm.

What's lacking in most corporate executives today is a sense of humor, which Newman excelled in. As Newman's Own website says: "Shameless exploitation in pursuit of a common good."

In the corridors of corporate America, nobody talks that way today.

9

SYMBOL

VISUALIZING THE INVISIBLE.

A verbal metaphor is a figure of speech in which a word normally used for one thing is applied to another.

"America is a melting pot."

A visual metaphor is a symbol that can bring an invisible product to life. How do you visualize "insurance," for example? You can't.

That's why insurance companies are big users of visual metaphors or symbols. These symbols can be strong visual hammers.

Travelers uses a red umbrella to symbolize the protection the company's insurance provides.

"It's better under the umbrella" is its latest verbal nail.

The history of the red umbrella demonstrates the enduring power of a visual. In 1998, in a misguided

effort to create a financial supermarket, banking giant Citicorp merged with the Travelers Group.

The combination was called "Citigroup" and the red umbrella was used to symbolize the group's "financial supermarket" concept.

The history of conglomerates is a dismal one and Citigroup was no exception. Four years after the merger, Citigroup spun off the Travelers in an IPO, but kept the valuable red umbrella as part of the Citigroup logotype.

Two years later, Travelers (minus the umbrella) was bought by The St. Paul Companies for $16 billion, changing its name to The St. Paul Travelers Companies.

Consider the situation back at the bank. Citigroup had been using the red umbrella as the symbol for its banking operation for many years. Yet the public still thought the umbrella meant "insurance."

Nine years after Citigroup started using the red umbrella, it threw in the towel and sold the red umbrella symbol to The St. Paul Travelers Companies. Which changed its name to The Travelers Companies.

Chief executive Jay Fishman said at the time: "The recognition of the umbrella to the Travelers name was really quite remarkable."

When a visual conflicts with a verbal, the visual always wins. Take a picture of a beautiful woman and label the picture "ugly woman."

Ugly woman

In spite what the caption says, viewers don't believe she is ugly, but just assume somebody put the wrong caption on the picture.

Not the wrong picture on the caption. The visual always dominates the verbal. Not the other way round.

The sale of the red umbrella to The Travelers left Citigroup and its other brands including Citibank, CitiFinancial and CitiMortgage without a visual trademark.

So the company created a red "halo" which I assume is supposed to be a symbolic red umbrella. But Citibank's red halo doesn't work nearly as well as Travelers' red umbrella.

A "red" symbol that works better than the red halo is the red hat used by Red Hat, Inc., a software company that dominates the market for Linux, the open-source computer operating system, the chief rival to Windows.

Linux is free, but Red Hat makes its money with support, training and integration services.

In 2013, the company had revenues of $1.5 billion and a net profit margin of 11.6 percent.

(Visuals that can be verbalized are stronger than abstract designs like the "red halo" that defy verbal explanations.)

Most high-performing sales people are sweet, pleasant and affable individuals. Not Flo, the spokesperson and the visual hammer for the Progressive Insurance brand.

"Irritating" is one of the milder things you can say about her.

As one consumer said: "I wish Flo from Progressive would comb her hair or get a new style...and lighten up the flaming red lipstick."

All of which would make Flo look better, but at the cost of memorability. And if your brand's symbol isn't memorable, then your message is probably lost, too.

"Discounts," Progressive's verbal nail, is memorable, too. That's particularly impressive because Flo didn't make her first appearance on television until 2008.

And Progressive is spending less money than two of the biggest auto insurance companies, Geico and State Farm.

In 2013, Progressive Insurance spent $587 million on advertising versus State Farm's $624 million and Geico's $1,014 million.

Geico's billion-dollar spending seems to be paying off. Its big budget and its visual hammer (the gecko, a reptilian mascot) have created a memorable marketing program.

Geico's verbal nail, "15 minutes could save you 15 percent or more on car insurance," is also quite memorable, thanks to repetition.

(Geico's massive advertising budget, which dwarfs that of the other major players, is partly responsible for its success.)

Geico has also used Neanderthal-like cavemen in a modern setting to promote its brand.

The nail, "So easy, a caveman could do it," was memorable, but not very motivating.

The real motivation is the 15-percent savings which is lost on cavemen who obviously don't care about savings on car insurance.

When the nail is weak, it's usually a sign that the marketing people picked the hammer first, which violates the basic marketing principle of nail first, hammer second.

Cavemen might make interesting television spots, but they lack a strong, motivating verbal connection. However, they were different. As a result, Geico's Cavemen even got their own short-lived TV show.

Both Geico and Progressive have been shaking up the insurance business. So much so that Allstate felt forced to respond.

In 2010, Allstate introduced "Mayhem," its visual hammer played by actor Dean Winters.

The brand's verbal nail, however, is a mess.

One version goes like this:

"You can save money and be better protected from Mayhem like me." In another version: "Mayhem is everywhere. Are you in good hands?"

In essence, Allstate now has two visual hammers (Mayhem and Good Hands) and two verbal nails.

The resulting confusion is never a good idea. This is particularly true for a brand whose name (Allstate) is often confused with the name of its leading competitor (State Farm.)

State Farm has a memorable verbal nail (Like a good neighbor, State Farm is there) but lacks a visual.

Its "three rings" logotype is a cliché that has been used by many brands in the past including Ballantine Ale.

On television, State Farm is turning its verbal nail into a "magic jingle." Sing the good neighbor jingle, point your finger and your wish will come true.

What makes good TV? Demonstration, action, motion … all the attributes of the State Farm commercials except one, a visual hammer.

State Farm doesn't have one. In the long term, that's a big mistake, especially for an invisible product like insurance.

Perhaps the oldest visual hammer in the insurance business is the "Rock of Gibraltar," used by Prudential since the 1890s.

The company's toll-free number (1-800-THE-ROCK) tied into the Rock of Gibraltar as well as various verbal nails: "Get a piece of the rock." And: "Strength of Gibraltar."

Time, however, has weakened the rock. It was a good symbol yesterday when print was the dominant medium, but not today.

When it comes to insurance advertising today, television is the dominant medium. The insurance industry spends many billions of dollars a year on television advertising.

Having a visual hammer that doesn't move is a serious handicap on television. That's one reason Prudential has been moving away from verbal rock metaphors.

"Growing and protecting your wealth" is a recent Prudential slogan. Sooner or later, Prudential will also need a new hammer.

On the other hand, Pacific Life has a hammer that works well on television. The humpback whale which represents qualities such as performance, strength and protection. The whale is an outgrowth of the Pacific Life Foundation, a nonprofit  dedicated to preservation and conservation of marine mammals.

The Foundation actually pre-dated the company's use of the whale in television commercials.

For more than 25 years, Snoopy and other Peanuts characters have served as visual hammers for the MetLife brand.

Currently, the company uses airplanes and blimps to animate its TV commercials.

While the Snoopy hammer 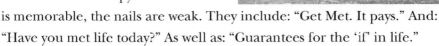 is memorable, the nails are weak. They include: "Get Met. It pays." And: "Have you met life today?" As well as: "Guarantees for the 'if' in life."

What's missing in the MetLife program and also missing in most of today's marketing programs is the notion of locking the visual hammer and the verbal nail together.

Often a copywriter selects a nail and an art director picks a hammer and the two never seem to connect with each other.

Like insurance, a lot of marketing time and money goes into selling pharmaceutical products, but while the pills may be visible, the visual hammers usually are not.

Or if they are, they aren't exactly appropriate hammers.

Take erectile-dysfunction drugs. The first brand in the category (Viagra) made a wise decision to pre-empt a color by using blue pills. What should competitors have done to differentiate their brands?

One of the oddest visual symbols is the twin bathtubs used by Cialis, a brand currently a close second in erectile-dysfunction drugs.

And the Cialis brand is widely expected to become the market leader soon.

The rise of Cialis is remarkable because it was the third drug in the category, after Viagra and Levitra.

(It's as if Royal Crown, the No.3 cola, suddenly became one of the cola market leaders.)

Why the twin bathtubs? Consider the situation from the company's point of view. There's no acceptable way to demonstrate the consumer benefits of an erectile-dysfunction drug.

But the twin bathtubs convey the idea of two naked people without showing them naked or even remotely exotic. The brand's verbal nail (the 36-hour drug) also differentiates Cialis from its competitors.

Baking soda is a widely-used household product and the No.1 brand is Arm & Hammer.

Its visual hammer is an old-fashioned arm-and-hammer logo dating back to the 1860s.

With inexpensive products like baking soda, a strong visual that is locked with the brand name makes the brand almost impregnable to competition. Take salt, for example. Morton salt has been the leading brand of table salt for many decades. Morton's visual hammer is a young girl with an umbrella walking in the

rain and scattering salt behind her. The nail: "When it rains, it pours."

According to one source, the Morton salt girl (which has been redrawn over the years) is one of the ten best-known symbols.

Morton salt's verbal nail, "When it rains, it pours," is not only a benefit of the brand, it's also a memorable double-entendre.

Car-rental companies provide a service that is deliberately invisible. Who wants to rent a vehicle with a Hertz logotype on it?

Hertz, however, is trying to increase its visibility with a mascot named Horatio, an animated dashboard figurine with a football-shaped head.

Unfortunately, the verbal nail, "We're at the airport and in your neighborhood," is one of the blandest slogans ever developed.

Horatio is not wacky enough to be memorable and his connection to car rentals is almost nil. (Hertz named Horatio after Horatio Jackson, one of the first people to drive a car across America.)

Symbols, whether they are used as visual hammers or not, play an important role in today's society. On products, on websites, on clothing, on retail stores and on billboards.

The Swoosh, for example, identifies a Nike product in situations where the Nike name might not be readable. Like on a shoe or on a hat.

Instead of developing a recognizable symbol, too many companies take the easy way and use initials instead.

Who makes the "N" shoe? People probably don't know.

But most people can readily figure it out. But it still takes a while to come up with the brand name, "New Balance."

Here's the difference. When you see the Swoosh on a shoe, the Nike name instantly registers in your mind.

When you see the letter "N," you have to think about it for a while to come up with the name. And most people don't bother to do so.

When you have more than one name, you need all your initials if you have any hope of widespread consumer recognition. In fast food, "M" stands for McDonald's, but could "B" ever stand for Burger King?

Embassy Suites uses the letter "E" on its hotels and on its vehicles. But the street visibility of the Embassy Suites hotel chain might be improved by using two initials instead of one.

Human minds think in words. If Face Book was the brand's name, it should have used "fb" as a symbol.

EMBASSY SUITES HOTELS

But the single word Facebook allows the site to just use "f" as the visual for its button and its icon.

Where the brand has the space, Facebook wisely uses its name and singular blue color for its visual hammer. It's almost always better to use words than initials.

A tree is a simple shape. One of the most effective visual hammers is the tree used by the Pebble Beach Company as a corporate trademark.

The tree is a drawing of the iconic "Lone Cypress" tree.

Not only is the tree symbol memorable for the Pebble Beach

PEBBLE BEACH
COMPANY

Company, but it also deflects consumer attention from the literal meaning of the name, Pebble Beach.

After all, consumers prefer sand beaches, not pebble beaches.

With a name like DoubleTree, it's logical the hotel chain would use two trees as its trademark

But the chain has reversed the normal order of things.

You have to read the name (DoubleTree) before you can identify these symbols as trees.

To the average consumer, the "trees" look more like ping-pong paddles.

Recently, the DoubleTree hotel chain changed its logotype. The new design demonstrates how verbally-oriented DoubleTree management has become. Instead of two trees, the DoubleTree trademark now has one tree and one "D."

If your name is DoubleTree how can you show just one tree? And then show the tree before the

letter D? As if the name were TreeDouble. That's backward thinking.

This is not a visual that instantly communicates a message. This is a mash-up that needs to be decoded. Let's see, a tree and a D.

What could the "D" stand for? Dogwood? Dutch elm? Or maybe the color brown means that it's a "dead" tree?

Aah, I have it. DoubleTree.

That's not good enough. A visual hammer needs to be perceived by consumers in a blink of the eye. A visual hammer is not a puzzle to be solved by the prospect.

Compare Tommy Bahama's logotype with DoubleTree.

Not only is the Tommy Bahama

tree a visual symbol for the brand, but the tree is obviously a palm tree, the perfect visual for a "Bahama" brand.

10

CELEBRITY

PROS & CONS.

A marketing message can't be all message and no come-on.
You need to do something to get consumers to pay attention
to what you have to say. A celebrity can often fill that role.

Nobody, but nobody was as good as Bill Cosby in delivering
an advertising message.

In his 2011 induction into the American Advertising Federation's
Hall of Fame, Mr. Cosby received the "President's award for lifetime
contributions to advertising."

What made Bill Cosby so
effective? In a word: sincerity.

Consumers are remarkably
able to detect celebrities who
are just "mouthing the words"

as opposed to celebrities who seem to believe in the merits of the brand.

Bill Cosby's best work was for Jell-O pudding products, emphasizing
key phrases like "Yummy for the tummy" and "Thank you, mother dear,"
sounding just like some young kid enthralled with the idea of having
Jell-O pudding for dessert. Bill Cosby is exactly the kind of celebrity you
should be looking for when you launch a new brand.

Cosby also did memorable work for many other brands including Crest, Kodak, Coca-Cola and Ford.

Too many marketing people hesitate using celebrities because consumers know celebrities get paid for their endorsements.

That's understandable, of course, but can be overcome by a celebrity who can project absolute sincerity. As Bill Cosby once said: "I want to make the program interrupt the commercial."

But there are also three reasons to not use a celebrity as your visual hammer: (1) Celebrities are expensive, and (2) Celebrities aren't always credible consumers of your product, and (3) Celebrities are human and subject to human frailties that could damage your brand.

Witness the rash of negative publicity about Tiger Woods, Kobe Bryant, Charlie Sheen, Lindsey Lohan, Britney Spears, Martha Stewart, Mel Gibson and most recently Bill Cosby.

It's always a risk to hire a celebrity as a spokesperson for your brand. Then there's the expense problem. In the 15 years before Tiger Woods ran into trouble, he earned $951 million in endorsements.

That's an average of $63 million a year.

Then there's the credibility problem. Take Tiger's endorsement of Buick automobiles. On the surface, this seems like a good idea.

A young, charismatic, world-class athlete drives a Buick.

How could this not improve the perception of the brand?

But wait. In addition to making more money than any other athlete in the world, Tiger Woods also owns a $20-million, 155-foot yacht.

And several years ago, he paid $40 million for a 10-acre property on Florida's Jupiter Island and promptly tore down the house.

In its place, he built a new mansion, including two pools, a hundred-foot running track, a 5,000-sq.ft. gym and a four-hole golf course.

And he drives a Buick? Highly unlikely.

As you might have expected, Tiger Woods' endorsement of Buick from 2002 to 2008 failed to work in the marketplace.

Buick sales in America declined dramatically. From 432,017 vehicles in 2002 to 137,197 vehicles in 2008, a decline of 68 percent.

Another point. If Tiger Woods endorses Buick, who's left to endorse General Motors' top luxury brand, Cadillac?

God?

Cadillac's trademark is attractive, but what does the trademark say? It's just another take on heraldry, a coat-of-arms design that seems out of place on an automobile.

It's a stretch, but Tiger in a Cadillac is definitely a plausible endorsement. To many people, the best domestic cars are on par with the best European and Asian cars. So Tiger drives the "best" American car. A Cadillac, of course.

That's why Tiger's endorsement of Nike, the No.1 athletic-shoe brand in the world, makes sense. But suppose he had endorsed Reebok or Adidas instead? Would that have worked? Of course, not.

You need to be consistent. The world's best athlete (Tiger Woods) needs to be coupled with a strong leader brand. Not Buick or Reebok.

It's also why Tiger Woods was a good choice for Accenture, one of the world's leading technology and consulting companies.

Unlike shoes, consulting firms like Accenture provide an invisible service. Celebrities like Tiger Woods can visualize the invisible.

In the six years that Tiger Woods was the visual hammer for the Accenture brand, he greatly improved its visibility.

Revenues also increased from $13.4 billion in 2003 to $23.2 billion in 2009, an increase of 73 percent. In those same six years, Accenture's biggest competitor (IBM) increased its revenues only 12 percent.

After an athlete leaves the field, he or she is often quickly forgotten, but not always. A good example is John Madden and "Madden NFL," an American football video-game developed by EA Sports.

First introduced in 1988, the game has sold more than 85 million copies, racking up sales of more than $3 billion.

Although retired in 2009 as a broadcaster, John Madden still lends his name to the video game. Will Madden NFL outlive its spokesperson?

There's no reason it can't. Madden is a brand like Paul Newman, Orville Redenbacher and Coco Chanel.

Properly nurtured, a brand can live almost forever.

Isaiah Mustafa only made the practice squad of an NFL team, but he became famous as "The man your man should smell like."

Mustafa is the spokesperson for Old Spice, a Procter & Gamble brand that has been around since 1938. There's no question that Mustafa energized the old-fashioned deodorant brand. Sales skyrocketed after Isaiah Mustafa videos appeared on the Internet and went viral.

Mustafa became the poster boy not only for Old Spice, but also for social media. He generated millions of unique views as well as a lot of online activity with tweets and blogs. Marketing people went gaga about how Old Spice had reinvented itself.

The real question is, What comes next? And that's always a major problem for a brand like Old Spice with no real connection with its young, handsome spokesperson.

Even the brand's trademark (a sailing ship) is inconsistent with a guy who is more likely to be riding a motorcycle than a 12-foot dinghy.

The verbal idea of Old Spice, however, is strong. "Smell like a man." This reinforces the heritage of the brand and serves as a direct attack on Unilever's Axe, the successful fragranced body spray.

Teenage boys bathe in Axe with the hope of attracting teenage girls. Unilever advertising has humorously labeled this as: "The Axe Effect."

Years ago, 15-year-old Brooke Shields created a similar sensation with her television commercials featuring Calvin Klein's brand of jeans.

"Nothing comes between me and my Calvins" was the campaign's memorable verbal nail.

As sensational as Calvin Klein advertising was, it was obvious a teenager like Brooke Shields would eventually get older and outgrow her ability to project the right blend of innocence and sexuality in television commercials.

In the fast-moving fashion category, it probably doesn't matter. Over time, many fashion brands tend to become obsolete. Or the brand just moves on to the next hot model or celebrity.

Calvin Klein moved his brand to Marky Mark Walberg & Kate Moss and striped them both down to demonstrate their underwear and their bodies. And recently he moved on to Justin Bieber.

Can an endorser be too old?

Who won the 2010 Super Bowl? You might remember the New Orleans Saints won the football game but do you remember who won the advertising game?

It was the television actress Betty White.

According to USA Today, the Snickers TV commercial featuring the
88-year-old actress playing football
was the most popular ad on the
Super Bowl. Theme: "You're not
you when you're hungry."

If there is one critical thing
you need to know about marketing,
it is this: Marketing is not a short-term fix. (If you need to do something
in the short term, run a sale.) Marketing is a long-term proposition.
Don't think in years, think in decades.

Unfortunately, Betty White is not in a long-term position to endorse
the Snickers brand. But even worse, where is the connection between
Betty White and a candy? There isn't any.

It was one funny commercial that did little for the brand.

One of the best examples of the value of long-term consistency
involving a celebrity is Charmin toilet tissue and Mr. Whipple.

For 25 years (from 1965 to 1990) Dick Wilson played the role of Mr.
Whipple, the retailer who couldn't
stop himself from squeezing the
Charmin toilet tissue.

In his long career, Dick Wilson
did 504 separate television spots
promoting the Charmin brand.

(At one stage of the Charmin advertising campaign, Mr. Whipple
was named the third best-known American celebrity, just behind
Richard Nixon and Billy Graham.)

Charmin is also a good example of the value of a narrow focus.
The long-time market leader in toilet tissue was Scott Paper Company
(now owned by Kimberly-Clark) which started manufacturing toilet
tissue in the late 19th century.

But Scott couldn't resist line-extending its brand.

So in addition to toilet tissue, the Scott Paper Company introduced
Scott towels, Scott napkins and Scotties (facial tissue.) But something
happened in 1957 that would seriously affect the Scott brand.

That was the year Procter & Gamble bought the Charmin Paper Company. Not surprisingly, the Charmin family of products included paper towels, paper napkins, facial tissue and toilet tissue, the same range of products made by Scott.

But in those days Procter & Gamble was run by marketing people, not by management types.

So in a classic "narrow the focus" strategy, Procter & Gamble discontinued all Charmin products except toilet tissue and then hired

Mr. Whipple to promote the brand.

And instead of promoting all the features of its toilet paper, P&G focused on softness.

"Please don't squeeze the Charmin" was the verbal nail to the Mr. Whipple visual hammer. And the humor evolved around Mr. Whipple's inability to resist squeezing the tissue himself.

The Charmin brand has been the toilet-tissue leader for decades. Recently, Charmin had 30 percent of the market with Scott in third place with just 12 percent.

Another long-running advertising campaign featuring a celebrity was Maytag's "Lonely Repairman."

Launched in 1967, Jesse White was the character actor who played

the part of the Lonely Repairman, replaced in 1989 by Gordon Jump and in 2007 by Clay Earl Jackson.

For a number of years, Maytag was the largest-selling washing-machine brand in the country.

As one frustrated Maytag competitor said: "Their machines cost the same to make, break down as much as ours, but they get $100 more because of the reputation."

How can you visualize the reliability of a washing machine? You can't. So most brands use verbal approaches. Except Maytag.

Even a totally-absurd concept (Our repairman is lonely because a Maytag washer is so reliable it doesn't need service) can be turned into an effective campaign because it can be visualized.

Did you ever see a marketing plan with pictures or illustrations? I haven't. A marketing plan is usually nothing but words.

In the future, marketing plans are likely to include visuals along with the words. Take O, the Oprah Winfrey magazine, the most successful publication launched in the last two decades.

Current circulation of the magazine is more than two million.

No publisher would say that using the Oprah name on a magazine wasn't a good idea. But how many of these publishers would have taken the next step: Using Oprah's picture on the cover of every issue?

That's the visual hammer that accounts for much of the success of O magazine. On the other hand, not using Oprah on most of the OWN (Oprah Winfrey Network) television shows is what partly accounts for the network's lack of success.

Sometimes, however, the use of a celebrity can actually damage a brand. Especially when the person chosen is the exact opposite of what the brand stands for.

Take Dell. Back in 2000, the company was eager to get into the consumer market to complement its leadership in business computers.

Not a good strategy, but what was worse was the verbal nail and the visual hammer the company chose for the launch of its consumer line.

"Dude, you're getting a Dell" was the verbal nail in a series of TV commercials starring Ben Curtis, a 21-year-old college student.

(It didn't help Dell's image that three years later, Benjamin Curtis was arrested for criminal possession of marijuana.)

Dell sells its products primarily to businesses, not consumers. Even today, more than a decade after the Ben Curtis campaign, consumers represent only 20 percent of the company's total sales.

What do you suppose corporate computer buyers thought when they saw Ben Curtis hawk Dell products to consumers?

Suppose the chief executive of a major corporation asked his or her IT manager, "What kind of computers are we buying?"

"Dude, we're getting Dells."

In a corporate environment, that's not an appropriate answer.

Dell used to be the world's largest seller of personal computers. No longer. Today, Lenovo is No.1 with H-P in second place.

One reason? Dell has lost its focus.

Yesterday, the Dell brand stood for "direct sales to business." Today, Dell doesn't stand for anything except, "Just another company taken private because it couldn't make it as a public company."

If you study advertising history, you will find many celebrities (both real and invented) used in marketing campaigns.

Most of them last for a few years and then disappear. The companies that hire them are determined to do better the next time.

But the problem is not usually the hammer. The problem is usually the lack of an effective nail.

Dick Wilson did a marvelous job as Mr. Whipple, but what built the Charmin brand was the "softness" nail.

It was the ability to connect the two, the celebrity hammer and the softness nail, that were the essential ingredients in the brand's success.

And Jesse White, Gordon Jump and Clay Earl Jackson were believable Maytag spokespeople, but what built the brand was the "reliability" nail that made the Maytag repairmen lonely.

Pick the right nail and almost any celebrity will turbo-charge your brand. Pick the wrong nail and even George Clooney will have trouble getting your brand off the ground.

11

ANIMAL

ANTHROPOPATHY WORKS.

We often attribute human motivation to animals. Courageous people are "lion-hearted." Cowardly people are "chicken-livered." Greedy people are "piggish." Lawyers are "sharks."

People who are playful, but not serious, are just "horsing around." People who follow blindly are "sheep." People who gossip are "catty."

People who never give up are "doggedly" pursuing their dreams. People who seldom say anything are "quiet as a mouse." People who cling to the past are "dinosaurs."

Animals are also popular as pets in America. We own 86 million cats, 78 million dogs, 16 million birds and some 13 million reptiles. (My boys have one poodle and two hamsters.)

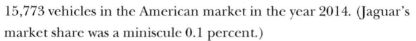

Because of our familiarity and love of animals, they can also make effective visual hammers.

Look at the visibility of Jaguar, an automobile brand that sold only 15,773 vehicles in the American market in the year 2014. (Jaguar's market share was a miniscule 0.1 percent.)

Compare Jaguar with some brands that sold more vehicles that year. Scion (58,009), Mitsubishi (77,643), Infiniti (117,330), Acura (167,843.)

The jaguar visual and the Jaguar name give the Jaguar brand more street visibility than many brands with much greater sales volume.

What's missing from the Jaguar marketing program? A verbal nail, of course. What's a Jaguar? Most people have no idea.

Take the high-end Nissan brand, Infiniti. Many people know the trademark for the Infiniti brand is a variation of the symbol for "infinity." But it's a weak visual device because it's used out of context (on a car instead of a mathematical paper.)

Sometimes out of context is all right, as long as there is some logical connection. But what is the logical connection between the concept of infinity and an automobile?

Does an Infiniti automobile run forever on one tank of gasoline?

A Jaguar automobile, on the other hand, looks like a jaguar animal. Sleek and fast.

A great visual hammer, but an almost non-existent verbal nail, seriously hurting Jaguar sales.

A BMW is the ultimate driving machine. A Porsche is the ultimate sports car. A Mercedes-Benz is the ultimate prestige vehicle.

But what's a Jaguar? It's a brand in search of a nail.

Another sleek-and-fast animal is the greyhound, the perfect symbol for Greyhound Lines, still the largest North American intercity bus company with 16,000 daily bus departures to 3,100 destinations.

Combined with the Greyhound visual hammer was one of the most memorable verbal nails in the history of marketing: "Take the bus... and leave the driving to us."

Today, however, the verbal nail has been modified and in the process has lost its poetry. "Go Greyhound and leave the driving to us."

To a logical left-brain executive, the new slogan might seem like an improvement, but it's not. "Go Greyhound" implies there are plenty of alternate bus companies you can choose.

"Take the bus" (and letting the visual communicate the brand) implies that Greyhound is such a dominant brand that nobody would ever consider choosing an alternative.

Greyhound Lines has also tinkered with its hammer, at one point adding red, white and blue stripes, perhaps to symbolize its focus on the American market.

Two symbols are never better than one. Two symbols only cause visual confusion. In marketing, simplicity and consistency always trump complexity and variety.

While a jaguar seems appropriate for a vehicle and a greyhound for a bus, what kind of animal would you pick for a $49-billion company that's into everything?

Television, theme parks, motion pictures and consumer products, among other things.

How about a mouse?

Mickey Mouse made his first appearance in the Walt Disney cartoon, Steamboat Willie. Since then, Mickey Mouse has been featured in some 120 Disney cartoons.

According to one source, Mickey Mouse is the most reproduced image in the world. Jesus is No.2. And Elvis is No.3.

Walt Disney once said: "I hope that we never lose sight of one thing: That it was all started by a mouse."

It's a hopeless task to try to find an effective visual hammer to symbolize an entire company.

Especially if that company is a conglomerate. A better direction is to look for the spark that ignited the brand.

General Electric, the company founded by Thomas Edison, inventor of the light bulb, uses symbolic filaments of a light bulb to spell the letters "GE."

Locking the visual to the verbal should be your No.1 objective.

One way to do that is by using a double-entendre. One of the best examples is the Merrill Lynch bull. The verbal nail: "Merrill Lynch is bullish on America," is one of the most-memorable slogans ever.

But what makes the slogan memorable is the visual hammer which instantly identifies the brand.

Merrill Lynch is bullish on America.

The lion is the "king of beasts" and could make an effective visual hammer, but it needs a verbal connection. Fidelity, a small banking chain in the South, uses a lion as its symbol and even owns the website lionbank.com. But the verbal connection is weak. Typical billboard: "Hunting for a loan?"

A clever headline, but not very memorable. You don't usually need to shoot a bank teller to get a loan.

If Fidelity were a giant bank, it could use a lion with the verbal hammer "King of Banks." (Look how effective Budweiser has been with a "King of Beers" approach.)

Next to the lion, the tiger is probably the most-admired animal. And Kellogg's Frosted Flakes has pre-empted the tiger.

In 1952, Kellogg's introduced "Tony the Tiger." The alliteration helped build the brand along with the verbal nail: "They're gr-r-reat!"

America's largest seafood-restaurant chain is not "Red Seafood," although that would have been a more accurate name since the largest seafood chain sells more fish and shrimp than it does lobster.

But the Red Lobster name is more memorable and lends itself to a more memorable visual.

The specific (lobster) is always more memorable than the general (seafood.) In the same way that the

specific (tiger) is more memorable than the general (animal.)

More than a hundred years ago, animal crackers were a popular treat for kids. A box of animal crackers contained a variety of animals like lions, tigers, bears and elephants.

Today, the most popular brand is Barnum's animal crackers produced by Nabisco Brands.

(The "Barnum" name refers to P.T. Barnum, the entrepreneur whose name is now enshrined in the largest circus company, Ringling Bros. and Barnum & Bailey.)

In total, over 54 different animals have been used by the brand. But a better direction would have been to focus on one animal.

That's what Pepperidge Farms did with its Goldfish brand.

Goldfish crackers greatly outsell the other animal cracker brands, although animal crackers are really more "cookie" than cracker.

In 1997, Goldfish crackers got an eye and a smile imprint added to tie in with its verbal nail, "The snack that smiles back."

Goldfish crackers are popular with parents of young kids since the snacks are baked and healthier. And kids love to see the little smile as they bite the heads off the fish.

Another company making the mistake of focusing on the general instead of the specific is Accenture. When they used a singular celebrity (Tiger Woods), the advertising resonated with the business community.

One can understand why they replaced Tiger Woods, but not why they chose an entire zoo instead of a single animal.

Its recent ads use a variety of animals including elephants, giraffes, polar bears, frogs, sharks and chameleons. (So far, no tigers.)

It's a mistake to use a variety of animals. A hammer is a singular idea. Multiple hammers for a single brand don't make sense.

Would it have made sense to feature a dozen different golfers in the original Accenture ads? I think not.

To create a memorable campaign it's better to focus on one animal. My choice would have been an elephant because it's consistent with Accenture's market.

Accenture's market is large companies. It once ran a print advertisement with an elephant on a surf board. Headline: "You're never too big to be nimble."

Integrating your animal hammer with your verbal nail is the key to marketing success.

Recently, Accenture dropped the animals in favor of focusing on clients like Unilever, Marriott and Royal Shakespeare Company.

Verbally, Accenture's move makes sense, but visually it does not. The animal visuals had some consistency and memorability.

But where is the visual consistency between this Warner Bros and Marriott hotel ads?

In the absence of consistent

visuals, Accenture is apparently counting on a prominent ">" symbol to unify its new campaign. That might make sense for an airline or an automobile, but it doesn't make sense for a consulting firm.

Cows might not sound like a good visual hammer for a chicken chain. Yet they work very effectively for Chick-fil-A, a phenomenally successful chicken-sandwich chain located primarily in the South.

Who is the enemy of the chicken sandwich? The answer is obvious. It's the hamburger sandwich, of course.

So for the last 16 years, Chick-fil-A has used cows in a humorous way to carry its marketing message.

A typical billboard shows cows with sandwich boards that read: "Eat mor chikin."

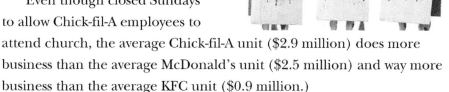

Even though closed Sundays to allow Chick-fil-A employees to attend church, the average Chick-fil-A unit ($2.9 million) does more business than the average McDonald's unit ($2.5 million) and way more business than the average KFC unit ($0.9 million.)

Even without a verbal connection to the brand, a visual symbol can greatly increase brand recognition, especially in a low-interest category like insurance and financial services.

Ever since 1974, Hartford Financial Services Group has used an elk as a symbol of the company.

The original Hartford television commercials featured an elk called Lawrence, a five-hundred-pound, ten-foot-tall animal with eight-point antlers and a thick red coat.

What an elk has to do with insurance was never mentioned in the Hartford commercials, but they certainly were memorable.

A better direction with a similar animal is what Deere & Company is doing with its visual symbol.

For 44 years, the world's largest farm-equipment company has used the John Deere brand and slogan: "Nothing runs like a Deere."

The company itself is 178 years old and very profitable with 2014 sales of $36.1 billion and net profits of $3.2 billion or a net profit margin of 8.9 percent.

Then there's the remarkable transformation of Aflac, the company that brought us the duck. In the year 2000, the company had a name recognition of 12 percent. Today it's 94 percent. And sales have gone up just as dramatically.

Aflac sales in the American market went up 29 percent the first year after the duck arrived. And 28 percent the second year. And 18 percent the third year.

When considering a visual symbol, you also need to consider the medium you propose to use. Television is primarily an entertainment medium while radio, newspapers, magazines and the Internet are primarily information media.

Information media work well with "news type" advertising messages, but television messages should contain entertainment elements or they are likely to be ignored.

Take StarKist, the No.1 brand of canned tuna. For many years, its TV spots featured Charlie, a tuna dressed as a hipster with a fisherman's hat and glasses.

According to Charlie, he has "good taste" and thus is perfect tuna for StarKist. But Charlie is rejected with a note attached to a fish hook that says, "Sorry, Charlie."

The reason: StarKist is not looking for a tuna with "good taste," but rather for tuna that "taste good."

It's interesting, too, that the No.2 brand of tuna (Bumble Bee) and the No.3 brand of tuna (Chicken of the Sea) also use animals to symbolize their brands.

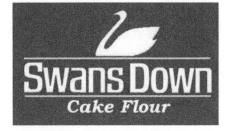

Many other food brands also link their names to animal visuals, including Swans Down, the leading cake flour since 1894.

Gorilla Glue goes one step further by locking its name with both its gorilla visual and its verbal. "The toughest glue on planet earth" is the verbal nail for the brand.

Vlasic, the leading pickle brand, uses a stork as its visual symbol. But without a real connection to the name, without a verbal nail and without a large advertising campaign, Vlasic's stork is losing much of its effectiveness.

As advertising costs continue to climb, more and more traditional brands like Vlasic are being forced to cut back on their ad budgets.

No brand can afford to rely only on advertising to sustain its visual hammer. A visual hammer has to be able to stand on its own.

That's why it's important to develop a visual/verbal strategy that will work effortlessly on your package as well as your marketing material.

Take Yellow Tail, an Australian wine introduced in the U.S. market in the year 2001. Three years later, Yellow Tail became the largest-selling imported wine, a notable achievement considering the fact that there are 6,500 imported wines on the American market.

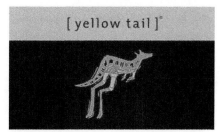

The Yellow Tail visual hammer is a black-and-yellow rendering of a yellow-tailed wallaby (a smaller cousin of a kangaroo) on the label.

Its advertising featured many different objects with yellow tails.

Typical headline: "Yellow Tail. Now spotted outside Australia." Some of the objects included a mermaid, a kangaroo, a lobster

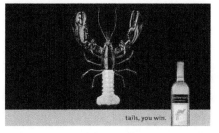

a peacock, a bird, and an alligator. I question the wide variety of visuals.

It might have been even more effective to focus on the wallaby only.

But there's no question the Yellow-Tail advertising and packaging built a strong brand, in part because there was little competitive imported-wine advertising during the early part of the last decade.

Recently, Yellow Tail has shortened its verbal nail to the innocuous slogan: "Tails, you win."

Dropping "Australia" is a mistake. A liquor brand need a "country of origin" to communicate its authenticity.

Scotch from Scotland is highly valued around the world. But Scotch from Switzerland? That doesn't make sense.

Saki from Japan. Tequila from Mexico. Champagne from France. Vodka from Russia. Rum from Cuba. A "country of origin" is helpful in positioning a liquor brand.

Not only did Yellow Tail build a wine brand that can last for decades, but it also helped improve the perception of Australia as a country that produces excellent wines.

Like wine, bottled water is another category with hundreds of brands fighting for market share.

PepsiCo's Aquafina and Coca-Cola's Dasani are category leaders. And Evian is solidly entrenched at the high end. One brand recently

making progress is Deer Park, a Nestlé brand. It's one of the few water brands that have a recognized symbol.

Consider some other middle-level brands: Arrowhead, Crystal Geyser, Poland Spring, Ozarka. How would you visualize them?

The one brand that could be visualized is Arrowhead, but the symbolism is faulty.

What does an arrowhead have

to do with water? Nestlé verbalized the brand as "mountain spring water" and uses a mountain range as a visual, an idea pre-empted by Evian.

In over-branded categories like bottled water, it's difficult to develop a unique verbal nail. That's why it's important to use a brand name like Deer Park that can be symbolized with a unique visual. Locking name and visual together can pay big dividends in the long run.

What often happens, however, is a lack of coordination between the brand name, the visual hammer and the verbal nail. Confusion has killed more branding concepts than almost any other factor.

Take Hamm's, a regional beer brewed in Minnesota, originally by the Hamm family which accounts for the brand's name.

Two brilliant advertising ideas built the Hamm's beer brand. The first was a jingle accompanied by the beating of tom-tom drums.

From the land of the sky blue waters.

"From the land of sky-blue waters." The second was Sascha, the bear. A dancing black-and-white cartoon bear.

Sascha, the bear, was so popular it was used by Hamm's beer for more than three decades.

After a sequence of owners, Hamm's beer is now being marketed by MillerCoors, but it's not the brand it used to be. It's now a cheap beer found on the bottom shelf.

Too bad. Hamm's beer could have become another "Coors" with a consistent visual/verbal strategy.

Like many other brands, Hamm's name was unrelated to its visual hammer (Sascha, the bear) and unrelated to its verbal nail (From the land of sky-blue waters.)

As the number of brands proliferate, as life gets more complicated, it becomes more important to lock all three elements together.

Three great ideas are not better than one good, coordinated idea. As society becomes more mobile, as people travel to places they might not have visited before, the need for visual hammers has intensified.

Take the retail industry. Most retail chains identify their outlets by names only. Preferably the larger the exterior sign, the better.

Some of the most successful retail outlets, on the other hand, use strong visual symbols to identify their brands. Colonel Sanders for KFC. A chili pepper for Chili's. A red lobster for Red Lobster.

Outback was the first Australian steakhouse. You might have thought the entrepreneurs who founded Outback would have developed a visual symbol to identify the brand.

Outback should have emulated one of its competitors (LongHorn steakhouse) that uses a "longhorn" symbol to identify its brand.

Marketing deals with three items: (1) The spoken word, (2) The printed word, and (3) The visual. The mind responds to each differently.

When you hear the words "Outback Steakhouse," you quickly think "Australian steakhouse."

Not so when you see the words "Outback Steakhouse." To grasp the meaning of printed words, you need to perform an extra step. You have to translate the visual symbols represented by the type into aural sounds your brain can understand. That takes time and effort.

Visuals are different. If you are attracted to a visual because of its size, shape or its unusual character, it makes an immediate impression without the need for an aural translation. That's why unusual animals are usually much more effective than common ones.

That's also why the leading high-end delicatessen brand in supermarkets is not called "Pig's Head." It's called "Boar's Head."

Even though a boar is nothing but a wild pig, a boar with protruding tusks is a unique visual which makes the brand memorable.

Nor is the literal meaning of the Boar's Head brand name much of a handicap. (The head is one animal part that is seldom eaten except for perhaps Andrew Zimmern on Bizarre Foods.)

A unique and distinctive brand name will develop a secondary meaning that allows consumers to associate the brand with a specific product category. Deli meat in the case of Boar's Head.

In spite of its lack of a verbal nail, Boar's Head is still a successful brand, thanks to its unique visual hammer.

When you can combine the name, the hammer and the nail, however, you can build a brand that is almost bulletproof. Roach Motel is a good example of a coordinated name, visual hammer and nail.

"Motel" is a common word, but what makes it particularly memorable is the fact that it is never used with a brand of insect killers. Then there's the killer nail for the Roach Motel brand: "Roaches check in…but they don't check out."

A penguin is an unusual animal which makes it a good choice for a visual hammer for Linux.

Even though Linux has only five percent of the PC operating-system market, the Linus brand name is quite well-known.

Linux's verbal nail is the brand's position as the most popular "open-source" operating system.

Compare Linux with Microsoft. How many people have a strong visual impression of Windows even though the brand has a 90 percent market share?

The Windows symbol is attractive but it isn't unique and different. Four squares is not much of a visual for a multi-billion-dollar brand.

In 2005, Google bought a little-known company called Android which had created software for mobile phones. On the heels of the iPhone, Google seemed ready pounce.

While launching its own phone didn't work out as planned, Google introduced Android as a mobile platform to compete with the iPhone.

Along with the technology is the Android visual, the green robot that has become a visual hammer for the brand.

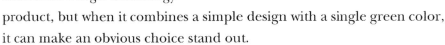

A robot might be an obvious choice for a high-technology product, but when it combines a simple design with a single green color, it can make an obvious choice stand out.

When it comes to Chinese food, a Panda is also the obvious choice. Panda Express was first in the mind and links the visual with the name, communicating both Chinese and fast food.

Currently, Panda Express is growing rapidly and is the leader in the Asian restaurant category with a 45-percent market share.

Fast-food restaurants and retailers, in particular, make a mistake in not developing unique visual hammers for their brands.

Retailers tend to be verbally oriented and often look at visuals as nothing more than "decorations for the brand."

Part of the reason for the rise of chains over local mom & pops is because the chains are more likely to develop visual hammers.

Not many local Chinese restaurants stand out visually the way Panda Express does.

The same is true when surfing the Internet. Websites need to create unique hammers to get their brands off the ground and into the minds of their prospects.

Hundreds of social networking sites have been launched in the past decade, but none have taken flight like Twitter.

Twitter picked a name that could be visualized and also focused on 140-character messages, calling the messages "tweets." Locking these three ideas together is a killer combination. Worldwide, Twitter has 288-million users.

Twitter has used various bird visuals, but wisely have settled on a simple image and a singular color.

((Maybe a dove is not the prettiest bird in the bush, but it is a very effective visual hammer.)

One of the more unusual animals used as a visual is the dodo, a huge bird distantly related to Asian pigeons.

Dodos existed only on Mauritius, an island which had no human habitation prior to 1598.

So it was a lack of fear and a child-like innocence that these birds greeted the first settlers who promptly killed them for food. By 1681, the last dodo had died on the island.

The dodo is the visual hammer of the Dodocase, a bamboo and cloth iPad cover constructed using traditional book-binding techniques.

The cover, available in black only, created a buzz among iPad users. When it came to thinking different, Dodocase certainly did.

Dodocase's verbal nail: "Protects from extinction."

Actually, it was the opposite. The dodo couldn't protect itself from extinction, but no matter. The mind just reverses the idea and accepts the Dodocase nail as reality.

Two good examples of the power of a visual to communicate rapidly are stop signs and stoplights.

The red color and octagonal shape of a stop sign communicates "Stop" before a driver can literally understand the word, "Stop."

And heaven help us if our stoplights were verbal instead of visual. If our stoplights said "stop, caution and go" instead of using red, yellow and green, the accident rates on highways would probably double.

Why do so many brands use a verbal approach and ignore the visual? It makes no sense to me.

Owners of these "verbal" brands should drive around our streets and highways for a while and perhaps they would see the light.

12

HERITAGE

PUTTING THE PAST TO WORK.

In 2003, in a metal storage bin in Wainscott, New York, 32 paintings were found that looked as if they were made by Jackson Pollock.

Wrapped in brown paper and tied with string, the paintings were labeled in a hand-written note as Pollocks from the 1940s.

Art experts have valued the Jackson Pollock paintings, if they are genuine, as worth $10 million. If not genuine, they are almost worthless. So it is with many products.

A Prada handbag you bought in a store for $1,800 might be worth eighteen hundred dollars.

A Prada look-alike handbag you bought on the street for $50 might be worth what you paid.

If you are careful where you shop, "fake" brands are not much of a problem today. But "pretender" brands are. These are brands that look, smell and taste like the big national brands, but nobody knows their names or what they stand for.

Supermarkets, drug stores, clothing stores and all types of stores are loaded with many "pretender" brands.

A "heritage" visual hammer can create authenticity for your brand and keep it out of the "pretender" category.

Consumers today are desperate for products that are truly authentic. Even a mythological character like Ronald McDonald can help validate

a brand. Kids in particular think Ronald is the guy who owns their favorite fast-food restaurant.

For kids between the ages of two and six, McDonald's is by far their first choice, often dragging parents, who might otherwise prefer Burger King or Wendy's.

What should Burger King have done about the powerful pull of Ronald McDonald?

Nothing. The best strategy is to ignore a competitor's strength and attack them where they're weak. Burger King should have focused on the adult market. (My dad once proposed that Burger King appeal to the teens-and-up crowd with a "Grow up to flame broiling" strategy.)

Instead, the chain emulated McDonald's by installing playgrounds and serving kiddie meals with toys. And to take on Ronald McDonald, Burger King introduced the King.

(The King, an anonymous character in a face mask, looks more creepy than cool.)

It's never a good idea to copy the competition and besides, the King is not a very good copy. Ronald is warm and fuzzy; the King is cold and distant. Not a good symbol for a burger chain.

Ten years ago in sales per unit, the average McDonald's outsold the average Burger King in the American market by 66 percent.

Today, the average McDonald's unit outsells the average Burger King unit by 113 percent.

In banks, like in burgers, size is an advantage. Big banks have more branches, more ATMs and greater street visibility than small banks.

There are some 7,000 banks in America, the most of any country in the world. But four big banks dominate the industry: Citigroup, Bank of America, JP Morgan Chase and Wells Fargo. Even though Wells Fargo is the smallest of the four, it's the most profitable.

Here are revenues and net profit margins for the four big banks in the past 10 years.

Citigroup . . . . $1,145 million . . . 7.0 percent

Bank of America . . . $1,101 million . . . 8.4 percent

JP Morgan Chase . . $1,010 million . . 13.5 percent

Wells Fargo . . . . $686 million . . 16.8 percent

A stagecoach is Wells Fargo's visual hammer, a symbol people will recognize from many Western movies including John Ford's classic film "Stagecoach."

Why use an old-fashioned stagecoach for a banking chain that is highly computerized?

In many marketing circles there's the perception that "old" is bad and "new" is good.

That's why "innovation" is the driving force at many of America's giant corporations. They want to be on the leading edge.

There's nothing wrong with innovation. "New" is good, but "old" sometimes is even better. "Old" can be the foundation on which to build a strong, up-to-date brand.

The "stagecoach" is a great hammer for Wells Fargo because it symbolizes a company that has been around for more than 150 years.

"Together we'll go far," the Wells Fargo verbal nail, is relatively weak, however. You won't go very far or very fast in a stagecoach. For that, you'd need an automobile or an airplane.

A better direction for Wells Fargo would have been to emphasize financial stability. "Other banks come and go, but Wells Fargo has been delivering financial results for more than 150 years," is the idea.

Wells Fargo was a real banking and stagecoach company, but a company or a brand can also be successful with a mythical concept.

A vaudeville song, "Old Aunt Jemima," was the original inspiration for an African-American character in 19th century minstrel shows.

So in 1889, a flour producer borrowed the name for a pancake mix and called it Aunt Jemima.

Today Aunt Jemima, owned by Pinnacle Foods, is the leading brand of pancake mix as well as a brand name used for syrup and other breakfast food products.

Intellectually, consumers know that people like Aunt Jemima were invented to sell products, but emotionally it's another story. And here is where a visual hammer plays an important role.

Emotionally the name and visual create the perception that Aunt Jemima was a real person and an exceptionally good cook. Otherwise, why would they have called the pancake mix, "Aunt Jemima?"

If the real Aunt Jemima was an invented name, there certainly was no Valley of the Jolly Green Giant and his familiar "Ho! Ho! Ho!"

And there definitely was no Betty Crocker or Pillsbury doughboy or Keebler Elves. It doesn't matter.

The Jolly Green Giant and the other symbols are visual hammers that humanize the brands.

They make the brands seem more real and authentic. They create an emotional bond with consumers that words alone cannot do.

At one point in time, Green Giant was the leading frozen-vegetable brand in spite of the fact that Birds Eye pioneered the category.

In the past decade or so, Birds Eye has recaptured its leadership, an achievement helped by its credentials as the first brand in the frozen-foods category.

Another factor that undermined Green Giant's frozen-vegetable leadership was the extension of its brand into canned vegetables, a classic mistake and an example of the superiority of the specialist (Bird's Eye) over the generalist (Green Giant.)

Another mythical creature that built a dominant brand is Mr. Clean, the fictional spokesperson for a brand that was launched in 1958.

Within six months of its creation, Mr. Clean was the No. 1 cleaning agent and inspired the longest-running jingle in television history.

Mr. Clean gets rid of dirt and grime and grease in just a minute.

Mr. Clean will clean your whole house and everything that's in it.

As successful as Mr. Clean has been, I don't think the next iteration of the brand is going to do nearly as well. Currently, Procter & Gamble is taking him out of the house and using Mr. Clean to open a national chain of car washes.

There are national gas-station chains (Shell), national car-rental chains (Hertz), national fast-lube chains (Jiffy Lube), but not national car-wash chains. That's an open hole in consumers' minds that will eventually be filled by some brand.

But, in my opinion, that is not an open hole that Mr. Clean can fill. The brand is too identified as a household cleaner, not as a car wash.

Too bad. Retail establishments located on busy highways desperately need visual hammers. They need to catch the eyes of motorists and instantly communicate the brands and products or services provided.

The Starbucks mermaid. Target's target. McDonald's golden arches. Wendy's pigtails.

But Mr. Clean? It's going to take a long time to convert a household cleaner into a visual hammer for a car wash. If ever.

Procter & Gamble should have studied the fate of Mr. Peanut when the Planters brand was line-extended into many snack foods, including pretzels, potato chips, corn chips and cheese curls.

A nut brand on a potato chip? That didn't make a lot of sense to most potato-chip customers.

That's the paradox of marketing. A weak brand name that means nothing can be line-extended into different categories. But who wants to do that with a weak brand?

On the other hand, a strong brand name like Planters that dominates the nut category can't be line-extended. And yet, strong brands are the brands that everyone wants to expand.

Created in 1916 by a Virginia school boy who won $5 in a contest for his drawing of a little peanut person, the Mr. Peanut character has evolved over the years.

Mr. Peanut, in my opinion, was absolutely necessary for the Planters brand to achieve its 40-percent market share.

Consider the name "Planters." It's generic. It's like "Growers" or "Producers" or "Farmers," all of which would be weak brand names.

Mr. Peanut, the visual hammer, makes Planters seem more like a specific brand rather than a generic name for a category.

He also humanizes the brand, always a good idea.

The Indian maiden on packages of Land O Lakes butter also helps to humanize the brand.

The maiden has undergone many minor modifications since she was painted in 1928.

The choice of an Indian woman turned out to be an excellent idea.

She communicates the natural purity of Land O Lakes butter.

Companies that launch new brands often makes the common error of using abstract images to communicate the idea that their brands are up-to-date and "with it."

Like the symbol for Panera Bread. Abstract art like this might resonate with art critics, but not with the general public who might think that, except for the word "Bread," the Panera logotype is for a brand of shampoo.

Actually, Panera Bread is a successful sandwich-shop chain. With 1,777 units and $2.4 billion in annual sales, Panera is the largest "bakery-cafe" chain in America.

But the brand itself could have been even stronger if it had a visual hammer. The current visual needs to be studied very closely in order to realize the lady with the flowing hair is actually holding a loaf of bread. Most people ignore the "arty" image and focus on the word "Panera."

Printed words need to be transformed by the brain into aural sounds before they can be understood. That takes time.

Because they can be recognized almost instantly, a visual hammer (in combination with a verbal nail) is superior to words alone

With some exceptions, the use of visual hammers to denote heritage seems to be a dying art. Instead, most managers want to modernize their brand's packaging.

Why modernize a package? Many marketers want to eliminate visual elements that might indicate that their brands are old or out of date.

But like fine Bordeaux wines, being around for decades is an advantage, not a disadvantage.

It must be good, thinks the consumer, if the brand has successfully withstood the test of time.

Take Pepsi-Cola which has been spending millions on packaging and new advertising to erase its 113-year history.

Even worse, the company recently introduced a "throwback" edition of its Pepsi-Cola brand, visually demonstrating the drastic changes that have taken place in the past decades.

Is that a good idea? Especially, is that a good idea to label the can, "Made with real sugar?"

That reminds consumers that current Pepsi products are made with high-fructose corn syrup.

Then there's the design issue. It's one thing to make minor design modifications, but Pepsi-Cola has pretty much abandoned its past.

The typography is different. The color is different. The logotype has been redesigned 11 times.

Pepsi-Cola used to be the No.2 cola. Today, Pepsi has fallen to third place, after Coke and Diet Coke.

Coca-Cola, on the other hand, has embraced its heritage.

The brand still uses the same Spenserian script hand-drawn in 1886, the year Coke was launched.

Today, Coca-Cola is the world's third most-valuable brand. How's that for progress? Or rather, lack of progress.

13

YOUR HAMMER

HOW TO FIND ONE.

Years ago, Bill Bernbach revolutionized the advertising industry by introducing the team approach.

Before Bill Bernbach, a copywriter worked on the copy and then turned the copy over to an art director to be "visualized."

Bernbach radically changed the system by assigning teams of two, a copywriter and an art director, and then had them work together to develop the strategy before they created the advertising.

These art director/copywriter teams elevated advertising to a level not seen before. Often called the Golden Era of Advertising and celebrated on TV by the Mad Men series, the team approach is still widely used in the advertising business today.

But you don't need to hire an advertising agency and an expensive art director and an expensive copywriter to get the benefits of a team approach for your brand.

Inside your head, you also have a team you can put to work. Your left brain is the copywriter and your right brain is the art director.

Unfortunately, your left brain is a know-it-all, overbearing dictator. It over-rules visual ideas created subconsciously by your right brain.

Your left brain is verbal. **Your right brain is visual.**

When your analytical left brain concentrates on a problem, logic tends to win over intuition.

Your right holistic brain still has a say, but it tends to be overshadowed by the boss on the other side.

As a result, most people wind up being totally verbal and analytical. They live in a world of words. They think in words; they write in words; they talk in words.

And thanks to the digital revolution, we are bombarded with words on a scale never seen before.

Worldwide, 180-billion emails are sent every day. On Twitter, there are 500-million tweets sent every day. There are now 150-million blogs and more than one-billon websites.

When you live in a world of words, you tend to see the visual world as secondary to verbal reality. Yet nature is visual, not verbal.

Take a walk in a park. Scuba dive in the ocean. Climb a mountain. This is reality and there are no words in nature. Words are useful devices created by people to communicate the reality of nature.

Photographs, illustrations and drawings are artificial, too, but they are a more direct representation of nature than are words.

Take this photograph of a baby. No matter how skillful the writer, no matter how polished the copy, words alone cannot capture the emotional impact of a photo.

Words alone cannot replace the emotional impact of the Marlboro cowboy, the Coca-Cola contour bottle and the Aflac duck. These and other visual hammers are creating some of the world's best-known and most-valuable brands.

Yet read a typical marketing plan. Dozens of pages and thousands of words with almost no mention of the role a visual hammer might play.

That doesn't mean words are not important. Words are important too, but they have a very hard time getting into consumers' minds without the driving force of a visual.

A visual hammer makes an emotional impact on the right side of the consumer's brain which motivates the left side of the brain to verbalize the idea and then store it.

Your right brain doesn't think in the normal sense of what we mean by "thinking." It reacts emotionally and involuntarily.

Our emotions are not logical. Try to explain what you mean by love, joy, heartbreak, danger, worry or fear.

The emotions are real, but difficult to verbalize.

Before discussing how to counteract the left brain's tendency to take charge of the creative process, it might be helpful to briefly review the history of visual hammers in marketing. There are three phases.

Phase one: The unrelated hammer.

Some examples: The eye patch for Hathaway shirts. Tony the Tiger for Kellogg's Frosted Flakes. The mermaid for Starbucks.

The eye patch, the tiger, and the mermaid are added elements, not germane to the brands themselves.

In the short term, unrelated visuals can be surprisingly effective.

For one thing, there's no need to use a visual symbol that has a logical connection to your brand name. The sky's the limit. Use the most shocking, unusual visual you can find.

In the long term because the visual is unrelated to your brand, your visual hammer will often lose its effectiveness unless supported by consistent and massive advertising.

Hathaway used to have a significant market share. Not so today. Ralph Lauren, has replaced it as the dominate shirt brand.

Phase two: The related hammer.

Some examples: The milk mustache in the "Got milk" campaign.
The Aflac duck. Geico's gecko.
Ralph Lauren's polo player.

But wait. Isn't a polo player
as much an unrelated visual for
Ralph Lauren as the eye patch
was for Hathaway shirts?

Not exactly. Anybody could lose an eye, but only wealthy people can
afford to play polo. The eye patch is a more shocking visual and perhaps
attracts more attention than a polo player.

But the polo player communicates the "upscale" position the Ralph
Lauren brand wants to occupy.

That's the difference between a related visual and an unrelated one.
The related visual does a much better job hammering an attribute.

Especially if the visual hammer is reinforced by a strong verbal nail,
something Ralph Lauren has neglected to do.

Phase three: The embedded hammer.

In the past, most visual hammers were added to marketing programs
to improve their effectiveness.

The latest, and most dramatic development, is the introduction of
visual hammers embedded in the product or service being promoted.

Some examples: The zigzag designs of Missoni. The white earbuds
of Apple iPods. The red soles
of Christian Louboutin shoes.

The dripping red-wax seal
on Maker's Mark bourbon.
The lime on a Corona bottle.
The watchband of a Rolex.

Embedded visual hammers are far more authentic than related or
unrelated visual hammers.

Does anyone actually believe Tony the Tiger thinks Frosted Flakes
are great? Or celebrities get a white mustache when they drink milk?
Or celebrities actually drink milk?

Furthermore, an embedded hammer will continue to work without a massive advertising campaign, although that's not always desirable.

While I strongly recommend the use of PR to launch a new brand (as advocated in our book, The Fall of Advertising & the Rise of PR), the opposite is true for an established brand.

Advertising is like insurance. Nothing protects an established brand better than a large advertising budget. Brands like Rolex and Nike and McDonald's and Coke are almost invulnerable to competition, thanks to millions of advertising dollars spent on their protection.

But what if you don't have the resources of Coca-Cola or Nike?

Then forget advertising, because unless you spend enough money to get above the noise level, you might as well spend nothing.

The good news is that an embedded visual hammer can help even a small company compete with the giants, no advertising required.

An embedded visual is so much more powerful than words alone that it can compensate for the lack of marketing resources by amplifying the power of every sign, website, brochure and tweet you do.

In spite of the effectiveness of the many visual hammers mentioned in this book, there are actually very few brands (in terms of percentages) that have developed and taken advantage of the power of a hammer.

Most brands today are being marketed with unspecific verbal claims. Like these verbal positions for companies starting with the letter A.

Aetna: We want you to know.

American Airlines: We know why you fly.

American Cancer Society: The official sponsor of birthdays.

American Express: Take charge.

AT&T: Mobilizing your world.

Audi: Truth in engineering.

Like most of the rest of the alphabet, these companies use verbal ideas that can't be visualized.

These verbal ideas have meaning, but because they lack visuals, they have little emotional impact and are not memorable.

Why does this happen? Why do many brands use purely verbal ideas with no visual hammers?

Typically, a company will develop a positioning strategy, alone or in conjunction with an advertising agency, that is expressed verbally.

After company management "signs off" on the positioning strategy, the next step is to execute the strategy with words, pictures, videos.

In other words, romance the verbal idea.

Stop right there. Before you even think about executing a strategy, ask yourself, what is the visual hammer? Most verbal ideas are impossible to visualize. How to you visualize: "We know why you fly?"

Without a visual hammer, your marketing program lacks the most powerful device in your toolbox.

Let me repeat. A visual hammer is the best and most-effective way to get inside a consumer's mind.

But 99 percent of all marketing programs lack one.

Yet, in spite of the power of a visual hammer, the nail is still more important. The nail, after all, is the objective of a marketing campaign. The hammer is only a tool.

In practice, how can you deal with the nail and the hammer, in order to develop an effective, unified marketing campaign?

First, use your left brain to express the essence of your strategy in a single word or concept.

Stop. If you're satisfied with your verbal concept, don't think about it anymore. Go for a walk, take a nap, relax in the shower.

Daydream for a while. Let your right brain go to work...without constant interruptions from your logical, analytical left brain.

Many great ideas can come to your mind not my concentrating on the problem but by relaxing and letting the solution occur to you.

The idea for the Absolut bottle campaign, one of the most-successful ad campaigns ever, came to art director Geoff Hayes in his bathtub.

So relax. Hopefully in an hour or two, a visual will occur to you without any conscious effort. That's the way the right brain works. Emotions can't be forced.

What if no visual idea occurs to you? Then it's back to square one. Try to find another verbal expression of your marketing strategy.

Often you need to sacrifice a proposed verbal position in order to generate one that can work with a visual hammer.

Take BMW. Years ago, it's easy to imagine that the company might have chosen "performance" as a positioning strategy.

That's logical and consistent with the favorable reviews of BMW vehicles in automotive magazines. But where is the visual hammer that can drive in a verbal nail called performance?

Instead, BMW chose "driving" as its positioning strategy, a verbal concept that could be visualized on television.

In practice, one soon learns why most marketing programs lack a visual hammer. Their verbal ideas are much too broad.

To develop a hammer you need a narrow focus you can visualize in a dramatic way.

Don't fret about narrow concepts not appealing to as many people as broader ones. Better to use a narrow concept to motivate a segment of the market rather than a broad concept that motivates no one.

It's become increasing clear that marketing is entering a visual era. Unless a new brand includes and embeds a powerful visual hammer, the new brand is unlikely to succeed. Paraphrasing an old proverb:

For want of a hammer, the nail was lost.

For want of a nail, the campaign was lost.

For want of a campaign, the brand was lost.

For want of a brand, the company was lost.

The nail is more important, but the hammer is more powerful. That's not an easy concept to grasp.

That's why I wrote this book.

About the Author

LAURA RIES

Laura Ries is a leading marketing strategist, bestselling author and television personality. Together with her father Al Ries, the positioning pioneer, she consults with companies around the world.

She is co-author of five marketing books that have become bestsellers. The 22 Immutable Laws of Branding (1998), The 11 Immutable Laws of Internet Branding (2000), The Fall of Advertising & the Rise of PR (2002), The Origin of Brands (2004), and War in the Boardroom (2009).

Visual Hammer, her debut solo book, was first published in 2012 as an ebook. It introduced the revolutionary principle that in marketing the visual is more important than the verbal. It has been translated into the Chinese, Russian, Turkish and German languages.

Her second book "Battlecry" now in production will complement the Visual Hammer book by outlining strategies for improving the effectiveness of a company's verbal nail.

In addition to her consulting assignments, Laura is a frequent guest on major television programs from the O'Reilly Factor to Squawk Box. She appears regularly on Fox News, Fox Business, CNBC, CNN and HLN.

And she is frequently quoted by the Associated Press, Bloomberg and The Wall Street Journal.

A resident of Atlanta, Georgia, Laura enjoys many outdoor activities such as horseback riding, swimming, skiing and triathlons.

Her website is: LauraRies.com. Her company's website is: Ries.com.

Connect with Laura Ries

Ries & Ries consulting: ries.com
About me: lauraries.com
Blog: riespieces.com
Videos: riesreport.com
Twitter: @lauraries
Facebook: facebook.com/lauraries
LinkedIn: linkedin.com/in/lauraries
YouTube: youtube.com/user/riesreport
Instagram: instagram.com/lauraries

Printed in Great Britain
by Amazon

35160277R00098